TO KNOW THE STARS
a simple guide to the night sky

by Guy Ottewell

The picture on the front cover shows the Earth and a person on it. She is drawn nearly a million times too large, otherwise we would not be able to see her.

She is looking at the sky with her telescope on a summer evening. That is, it's evening on the part of the Earth where she is standing. This part of the Earth—the eastern U.S.A.—has just moved around into the shadow of night, so that she is able to see the stars.

The stars toward the lower right are in the constellation called Sagittarius, the Archer. The bright star toward the top is Altair, in the constellation Aquila, the Eagle. The wide soft band of light going through this part of the sky is the Milky Way—really made of millions of stars too far away to be seen separately.

Farther to the left is the Moon. It has not yet "risen"; that is, it has not yet come into view for the part of the Earth where the person is standing. It will soon come into view, as the Earth turns. The Moon is 240,000 miles from the Earth, but it is much, much nearer than the stars.

ISBN 978-0-934546-69-0

2nd edition, September 2014
reprinted November 2014

To the children of the Montessori School
of Greenville, South Carolina. They enjoyed it!

Preface

This is a beginning book for young people—and others. It aims to satisfy as directly as possible the curiosity of children who would like to know the names and natures of the stars and what else is out there in the universe. It takes them out straight away under the real stars, shows them those that can be seen *now*, this month, and tells the stories that make those stars unforgettable. Afterwards, it explains, or begins to explain, the questions that will arise.

The main part of the book—the monthly pages—works with children down to elementary-school age. They will be growing mentally when they start drawing on the "More Explanations" that begin on page 54.

The book can be used by teachers; and, for beginners of any age, it is an easy doorway into astronomy. I know I have often picked up a "children's" book on some subject, such as spiders or volcanoes, when I wanted to get a rapid understanding undelayed by the cautions and epistemology of a scholarly book or article.

To Know the Stars grew out of *The View from the Earth*, which was a children's version of my large annual *Astronomical Calendar*. The earlier edition had no color and less than half as many pages.

The new edition has been enlivened with cartoons by Ian Dicks.

Where can the book be used? Many of the statements and diagrams are true for any part of the Earth, but others have to apply to a restricted part, simply because the Earth is round and not all its inhabitants can see the same sky or see things happening at the same time. Narrowly, the geographical area to which the book is adapted is the United States of America, around latitude 40° north. But the sky maps (the most essential part) show the way the sky looks for about this latitude all the way around the globe—southern Europe, central Asia, northern Japan. And things are not very different for a much broader band: the whole of the U.S., southern Canada, most of Europe—in fact, the thickly inhabited north-temperate zone of the Earth. Only in the arctic and equatorial regions and the southern hemisphere will the sky look very different. You will understand these differences by the time you have gained a fair understanding of astronomy. (The part necessary to understand is in the section called "On the round Earth.") And, for the further sections about the planets, Sun, stars, and universe, it doesn't matter where you live.

Universal Workshop
www.UniversalWorkshop.com

Raynham, Massachusetts, U.S.A., and Lyme Regis, Dorset, England

HOW TO START

It's a good idea to read this before you try the other pages. That way, you'll understand them better.

Going out under the stars

Is it dark outside? Is the weather good? If so, now is the time to begin. It doesn't really matter what time of year it is. (But it is better if the Moon is *not* shining in the sky.)

First, make sure you are dressed warmly. Even if it doesn't seem very cold outside, you will be keeping still, and that will lower your temperature.

If you are going to take this book with you, you will need a flashlight. But an ordinary flashlight will dazzle your eyes: after looking at the white pages, you will have to wait some time before you can see the stars well. The solution is to have a *red* flashlight. They are sold at bicycle shops; or you can put a red sock or a piece of red plastic over your ordinary flashlight. Red light does not dazzle the eyes as much as white light.

You will have to find a place that is as open as possible—without trees and houses standing close around. Also, get as far as possible from lights.

You can just lie on your back on the ground. That's what I like to do. Or lie on a blanket. Or bring one of those long garden chairs that unfold and tilt right back. Or at least find somewhere to sit where you can lean your head well back against something.

Just relax and gaze at the sky for a long time. No need to learn anything in particular yet; just enjoy the sight.

Constellations

The Navajo Indians say that the gods had all the stars on a blanket and had begun arranging them carefully in the sky, when mischievous Coyote came by. "Whaddya doing, pals?" he said—and

seized the blanket and flung it upward, so that the rest of the stars are scattered just anyhow.

And that's what it looks like: all irregular, but in a while you notice some patterns. You may find a line of three bright stars, or a cluster of faint stars close together, or some stars arranged in a shape that reminds you of a face. Groups like this are called "constellations." There are names for them. They are the way we find things in the sky.

Don't bother about learning any real constellations yet. If you like, you can imagine some of your own, and give them names, such as the Hammer, or the Cat, or the Long Straight Line—anything you like!

Continued on next page

Facing south

Now, let's get a bit more methodical. Instead of just facing in any direction, face **south**. Do you know where south is from your location? If not, you will have to stop for tonight, find out during the next day, and continue next night. Ask somebody where south is. Or you can find out for yourself: the Sun is south of you at mid-day.

Why is this important? Well, the constellations are quite difficult to find and recognize. And they move around. This is confusing enough. If you keep moving your position too, the constellations will seem to be on their sides or upside down, and

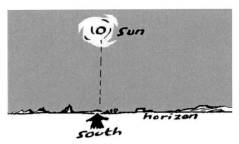

it will be even harder for you to recognize them. So it is best to make a habit of facing in one direction. South is the direction that works best.

Arches from left to right

Now, just lie watching for an hour, and see whether it's true that the stars do move.

It's like the hands of a clock: you can't see them move, because they move too slowly. You have to note the positions of some of the stars, by lining them up with trees or buildings or overhead wires. Then see where they are some time later.

You'll find they move like this:

Each star is moving to your *right*—from east to west. But they stay in the same positions relative to each other. It seems that the whole sky is rolling over toward the right.

It is very important to be aware of this movement of the sky. Make sweeping movements

with your arms, so that you really get the feel of it. Imagine what it would look like if speeded up.

The stars are always coming up into view from the horizon on your left, that is, on the east; we say that they "rise" in the east. Then they sweep slowly across the middle of the sky in arch-shaped courses. Then they "set," that is, go down to the horizon and out of view. They set on your right, that is, in the west.

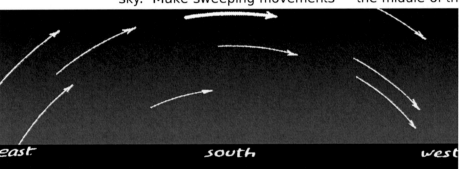

The dome of the sky

Now look at the larger picture of all this.

It shows *you*, lying on your back and looking up at the sky.

You are holding above you this book, open at the page for *the present month*. So you will now be able to understand the sky map for the month. It shows the stars where they are now. For instance, if this is January, you will see the group of stars called "Orion" in the middle of the sky map, toward the south. Looking at this same place in the sky, you will see the seven bright stars of Orion, high up in front of you, in the middle of the sky and somewhat toward the south.

Keep looking at stars marked in the sky map, and then finding them in the sky. Soon you will have identified many stars.

Of course the picture shows only a small bit of the Earth that you are lying on. And it shows the stars as if they were not very far away, painted on an imaginary dome over you.

The circles painted on the dome show the way the stars move as the night goes on. Now you can see why they seem to move in arches.

In 24 hours, a star will move all the way around. So, next night, you will see it again at about the same position.

Using the book

The sky maps show what you will see in the sky each evening (the early part of the night). They are the most important part of the book, or at least the part you should work with first. Each clear evening when you feel like doing some astronomy, keep looking at the *sky*, the *sky map for this month*, and the description that goes with it.

Then, any time you want to understand something that isn't explained there, look in the other pages at the end of the book.

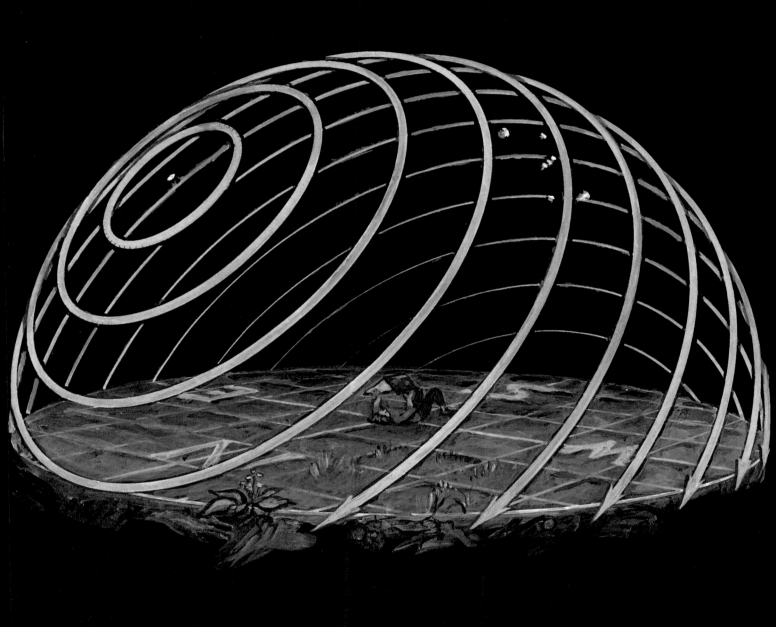

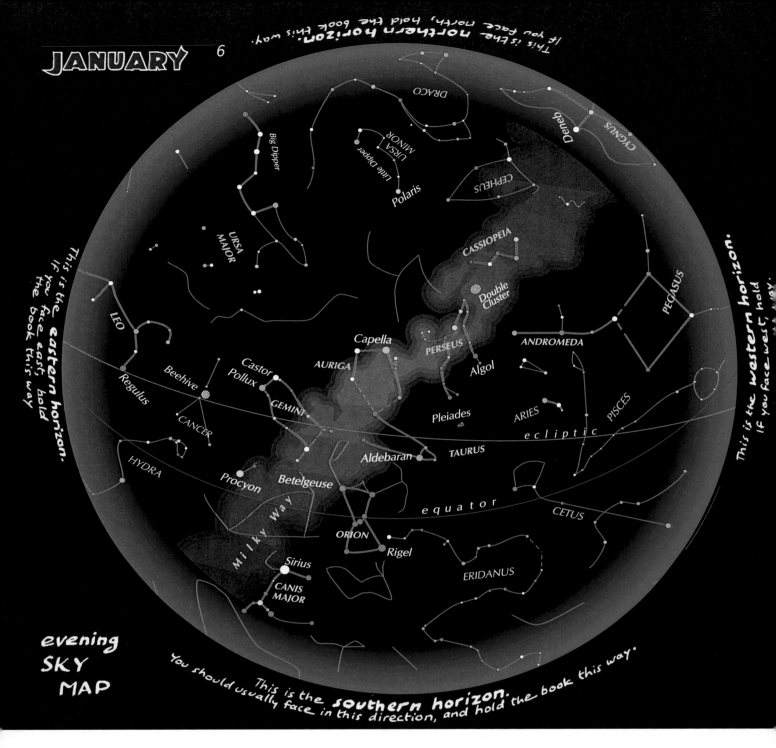

This is the eastern horizon. If you face east, hold the book this way

This is the western horizon. If you face west, hold the book this way.

DRACO

Big Dipper

URSA MINOR
Little Dipper

Polaris

URSA MAJOR

CYGNUS
Deneb

CEPHEUS

CASSIOPEIA

Double Cluster

PEGASUS

LEO

Capella

PERSEUS

ANDROMEDA

Regulus

AURIGA

Castor
Pollux

Beehive

GEMINI

Algol

Pleiades

ARIES

PISCES

CANCER

ecliptic

Procyon

Aldebaran

TAURUS

HYDRA

Betelgeuse

equator

CETUS

Milky Way

ORION

Rigel

Sirius

ERIDANUS

CANIS MAJOR

evening SKY MAP

Orion

The beginning of the year is a good time to start learning the constellations, because you can start with the easiest and brightest of them all. "Constellations" are imaginary pictures made of stars, and this one is a picture of a huge man called Orion.

Any winter evening, when it becomes dark, you will see him immediately, up there in the middle of the sky. His two shoulders and two knees are marked by four bright stars. Across the middle of this rectangle is his sloping Belt of three stars.

That makes *seven* very bright stars in Orion. No other constellation has so many.

One shoulder is a reddish star called Betelgeuse, and the opposite knee is a bluish star called Rigel. These are his two brightest stars. Look from one to the other and you will see the color difference.

Names like *Betelgeuse* and *Rigel* may seem difficult to learn.

Look at page 88 where there is help with pronunciation. When I first read about Orion I thought it was pronounced like OR-i-on, and I still rather wish it was! But people say o-RYE-on.

Down from one end of Orion's belt hangs his Sword, a line of three dimmer stars. The middle one of these is actually not a star at all, but a "nebula" or cloud of shining gas. In fact it is the most famous object of this kind, and is called the Great Orion Nebula. It

Taurus

Orion

Mintaka

Alnilam

Alnitak

the Horsehead (a dark nebula)

Orion's Belt and Sword

the Great Nebula

looks wonderful if you get a chance to see it through a telescope, or even binoculars.

Orion has three other parts, shown on our map by thinner lines because they are made of fainter stars. (If the sky is not dark you may not be able to see them.) He is raising a club with one hand, and a shield with the other; and he has a small head. He is a man of brawn, not brain!

In Greek legends, Orion was a great hunter. He boasted that he would soon rid the world of wild animals. The gods did not want this to happen, so they sent an enormous scorpion (a poisonous animal) to sting him. He died, but the gods were kinder to him after that: they put his picture on one side of the sky, and the Scorpion's far away on the opposite side of the sky. We will see this Scorpion and talk about it in July.

More about January ⟶

Taurus, the Bull

In his own part of the sky, Orion is still doing what he enjoyed: fighting with a more huntable animal, a wild bull. We call this bull Taurus. (*Orion* is the man's name, but *taurus* just means "bull" in Greek.)

The bull is charging down on Orion from up to the right. Actually the star picture is just of the bull's head. A triangle of stars represents his face. This triangular cluster is also called the Hyades.

One star in the triangle is much brighter than the others, and reddish. So we can think of it as the bull's angry bloodshot eye. This star is named Aldebaran. It is not really a member of the Hyades cluster, but is nearer to us, which is why it appears brighter.

The bull has two very long horns, which may be hard to see at first, because each is marked only by one star, at its tip. The horns together with the triangle of the Hyades make a shape like a capital *A* lying on its side.

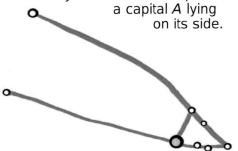

The Pleiades

Up to the right from the Hyades is another star-cluster, the Pleiades. It is smaller than the Hyades cluster, yet easier to see, because its stars are close together. This makes it very noticeable. When you are not looking straight at it, it seems like a little smudge of light, or a snowflake. In fact it may have been the first thing you noticed in the sky, even before Orion.

The Pleiades cluster is very famous. We call it part of the constellation Taurus, but for many peoples, such as American Indian tribes, it was a constellation by itself. It has other names besides "Pleiades." Many people call it the "Seven Sisters."

Can you see its shape? There is a little box of four stars. The brightest is at the upper left (it is called Alcyone). But the upper right corner of the box is really two stars. And outward from Alcyone is another star (called Atlas). That makes six.

So why the *Seven* Sisters? Since ancient times they have been referred to as *seven* stars. Is there a "Lost Pleiad"? People enjoy arguing about this, and the argument has never been settled.

If you have very good eyes, you may be able to see seven *or more* stars in the cluster. If you look with binoculars, you will see dozens; with a telescope, you will see perhaps a hundred! So really the six stars most people can see with their naked eyes are only the brightest members of the cluster.

Some people suggest that one of the stars may have become fainter, and that was why ancient people could see seven. Others say that ancient people often liked to count things in sevens even when there weren't really seven, because it was a sacred number.

The seventh brightest is a star very close above Atlas; we give it the name Pleione. In Greek stories, the Pleiades were the seven daughters of the giant Atlas and his wife Pleione. (So, if we give the names of Atlas and Pleione to two of the seven brightest stars, it means that *two* of the sisters are unaccounted for!)

We shall come all around the sky and back to the Pleiades at the end of the year.

A happening each January: the Quadrantid meteors

On any night in the year you may see a few meteors, or "shooting stars" as they are sometimes called. They are not stars, but bits of dust coming from out in space and flashing as they burn up in Earth's atmosphere.

There are several times in the year when, if you go out at night, you have a chance of seeing more meteors than usual. One of these special times is near the beginning of the year, about January 3 or 4. The "meteor shower" that comes at this time is known as the Quadrantids. To understand this you will have to read the section about **meteor showers**, on page 72, and then decide whether you want to stay out and watch for Quadrantids.

Hold the book 12 inches from your eye. Then this is how large Orion really looks in the sky.

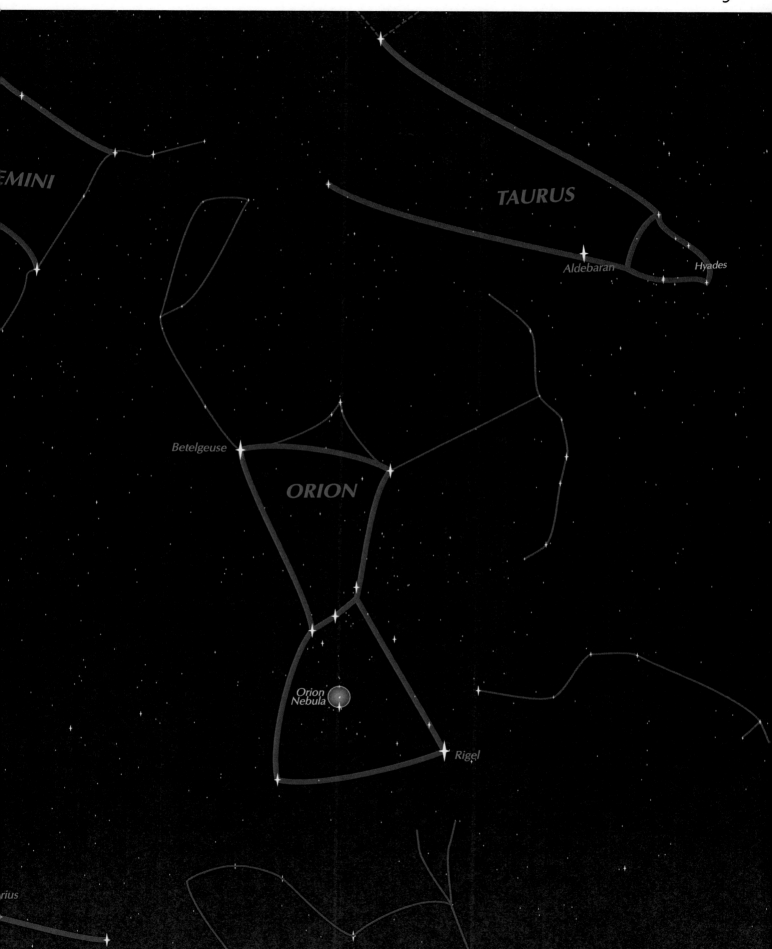

GEMINI

TAURUS

Aldebaran

Hyades

Betelgeuse

ORION

Orion
Nebula

Rigel

rius

FEBRUARY

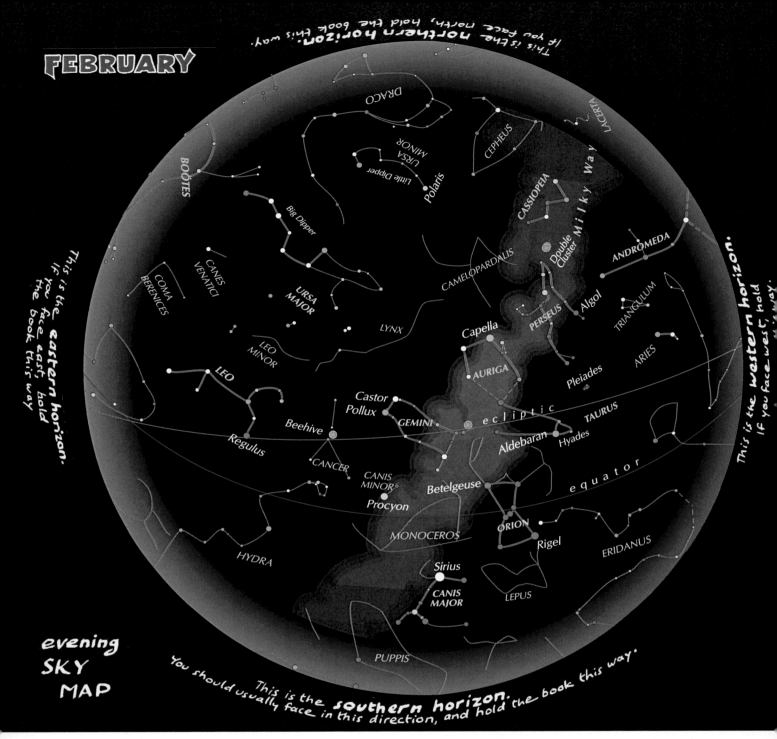

evening
SKY
MAP

The winter constellations

When we talk about "the winter sky," we usually mean the part of the sky we see in winter evenings, not long after sunset. The parts we would see around midnight, or in the morning before sunrise, are different; but at those times we are usually in bed.

The winter sky sparkles with bright stars. Many people notice this, without knowing why. Does it just seem this way because of the clear frosty air? No, the winter sky really does have more of the brightest stars. In the middle of it is a group of six glorious constellations. Last month you got to know two of them, Orion and Taurus. See if you can learn the other four this month.

Canis Major, and Sirius the brightest star

Orion's belt of three stars points down left (southeast) to Sirius. This name meant "scorching" in Greek. Sirius is the brightest star in the whole night sky, by far. (Of course the Sun and Moon are brighter, and so are some planets, comets, and meteors.)

When we say that Sirius is the brightest star, we mean it is brightest as seen from the Earth. It is really a bit brighter than our Sun, and is 8½ light-years away, which is fairly near for a star. There are other stars that are really much brighter, but much farther away. There are also a few stars nearer than Sirius, but less bright.

(What's a **light-year**? See "Distances," page 85.)

Like all stars, Sirius often twinkles. Also, as you watch it you may notice flashes of red, blue, and other colors. Really its light is white; the colors are caused as the light comes through the atmosphere of the Earth, like the colors of sunset. This happens with all stars, but is more noticeable with Sirius because it is so bright.

Sirius is the chief star of Canis Major. In Latin, *canis* means "dog," and *major* means "greater." Sirius looks like a stud on the dog's collar. The dog also has a foreleg, and three rather bright stars lower down forming his hindquarters, back leg, and tail. There are a few less bright stars from which you can make him a head.

These other stars in Canis Major are an example of what we just said about brightness and distance. They are all really much brighter than Sirius, but much farther away.

The dog is leaping behind Orion, who is already trying to deal with the bull Taurus on the other side. Let us hope that the dog is Orion's and is coming to help him, not to bite his heels.

The Milky Way

The Milky Way runs slopingly above Canis Major and Orion. Can you see it? It is a test of whether you have a good dark sky. The Milky Way is always there waiting for you. It is one of the most wonderful things you will ever see.

What is it? It is really billions of stars. Look at Sirius, the star that is so bright because it is "only" 8½ light-years away; then the stars around it that are farther away; then find others, fainter and fainter, and probably farther away. Gradually they merge into this background where they seem so faint and close together that you cannot tell them apart. Really they are about as far apart as we are from Sirius.

They are spread in an immense flat layer, like a pancake. This great pancake of stars is called a *galaxy*.

Canis Minor, the Lesser Dog

On the other side of the Milky Way from Canis Major is another dog constellation: Canis Minor, the "smaller dog." It certainly is smaller. There is just one very bright star, Procyon, and one other noticeable star, so the dog seems to have only a head and nose.

Procyon is a Greek name meaning "before the dog." (The *pro* part means "before"; *cyon* means "dog.") It got this name because it is higher in the sky than Sirius: so it rises into view first, and when people saw it they knew they would see Sirius soon after. At that time Sirius was the only "Dog" star; Procyon was just the star that is seen "before the Dog." Later people started thinking of it as a dog too; they are a pair of dogs, running on either side of the Milky Way.

Two more constellations for February ⟶

Gemini, the Twins

Straight north from Procyon is a very noticeable pair of bright stars: Castor and Pollux. The original Castor and Pollux were famous twin brothers in Greek stories. Castor was a wrestler and Pollux was a boxer, and together they went on many adventures. There was hardly any difference between them— except that Castor was mortal and Pollux was immortal. When Castor was killed, Pollux was so sad that he wanted to die too, but he could not. The chief god, Zeus, was so impressed by their brotherly love that he let them live together in the sky for ever.

Gemini is the Latin word for "twins." The two stars represent their heads; their bodies are the two ragged lines of stars sloping down to their feet, which stand on the Milky Way.

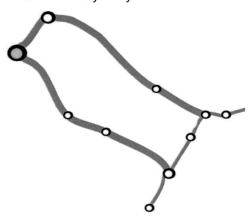

Pollux—the immortal brother—is slightly brighter, and is also a slightly orange color. In telescopes, Castor is more interesting: it is one of the many "double" stars in the sky. More powerful telescopes show that it really consists of *six* stars close together!

A cross-roads of the sky

The area over your head, in the middle of the sky on February evenings, is like a cross-roads.

You can see two lines crossing in it: the Milky Way, and the imaginary line called the ecliptic. Also, four constellations meet here. The feet of the Twins almost touch the club of Orion and the horns of Taurus. The fourth constellation, **right** overhead for people in the U.S., is Auriga.

Auriga, the Charioteer

Auriga is the Latin word for "charioteer," a man who drove a chariot pulled by horses. You need a lot of imagination to see a charioteer! The pattern of stars doesn't look like anything in particular. It has one very bright star, Capella. There is a star that could be the charioteer's shoulder, straight to the left of Capella; then another one straight downward, so that these three form one corner of a square. But the star that should complete the square is too far downward and outward to the right.

The name of Capella is Latin for "she-goat." Just down and right from Capella are three fainter stars called the "Kids," or young goats. So it seems that the charioteer is trying to drive his chariot while for some reason holding on his left arm a nanny-goat and her kids!

Though Auriga is a vague constellation, there is a way you can remember its position in relation to Taurus. Look at the star marking the tip of Taurus's upper horn. (It is brighter than the other horn-tip star, and is called El Nath, which means in Arabic "the butting" star.) This star is nearer to the stars of Auriga than it is to the other stars of Taurus's head. And if it were included in Auriga, Auriga would form a kind of five-sided box. Earlier astronomers did consider the star to belong to both Taurus and Auriga.

Leap-days

Can you remember how many days each month has?

One way is to count on your knuckles.

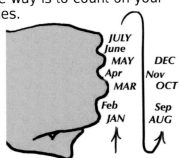

The knuckles are the seven long months, with 31 days each: Jan Mar May Jul, Aug Oct Dec. The dips between the knuckles are the five short months. They have 30 days—except February, much the shortest, with 28.

Why does February have only 28 days? Blame the ancient Romans. It's as if they didn't want a month at all in this wintry time, and wanted to get through it quickly!

Adding seven 31s and four 30s and 28, you get a year of 365 days.

But the years 2000, 2004, 2008, 2012, 2016 and so on are "leap-years." In these years an extra day, the "leap-day," is added to the end of February, and called February the 29th. So these years are 366 days long.

What's the reason for this?

The real year is 365.242 days. What do we mean by the "real" year? The time the Earth takes to go around the Sun. So it is also the real time between the seasons. For instance the middle of summer comes every 365.242 days.

Calling it 365 days might seem good enough. That was what the ancient Egyptians did. After several hundred years they found that their "summer" months had moved to winter! So the Romans introduced roughly the calendar we have now. By adding leap-days in some years, we make the *average* length of the year close to 365.242.

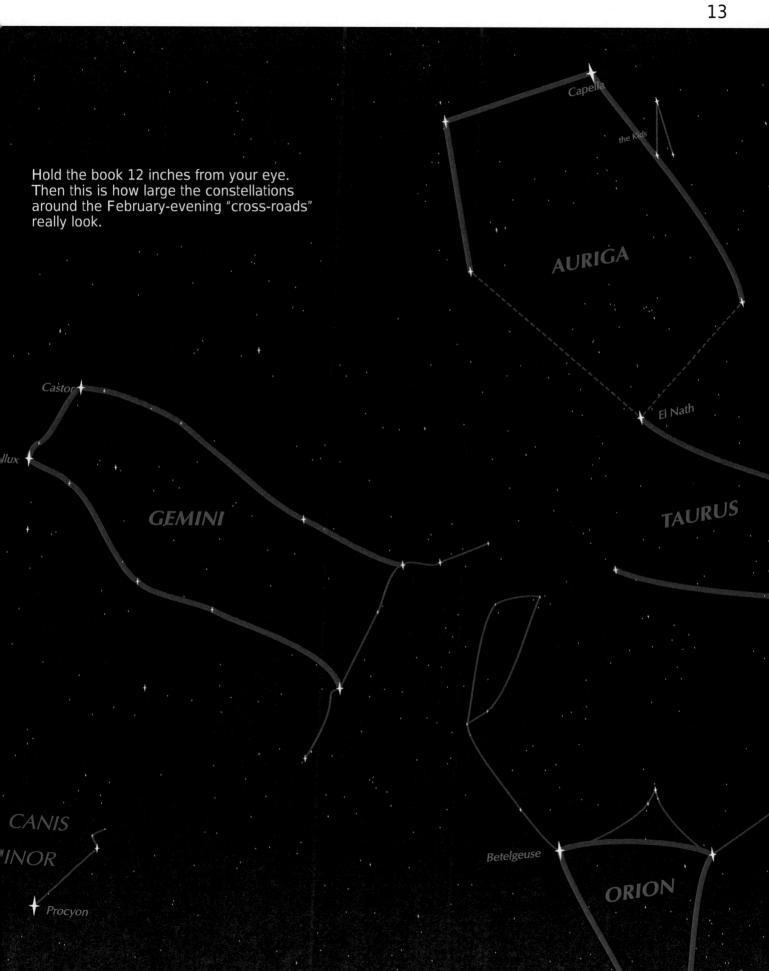

Hold the book 12 inches from your eye.
Then this is how large the constellations
around the February-evening "cross-roads"
really look.

Capella

the Kids

AURIGA

El Nath

Castor

llux

GEMINI

TAURUS

CANIS

INOR

Betelgeuse

ORION

Procyon

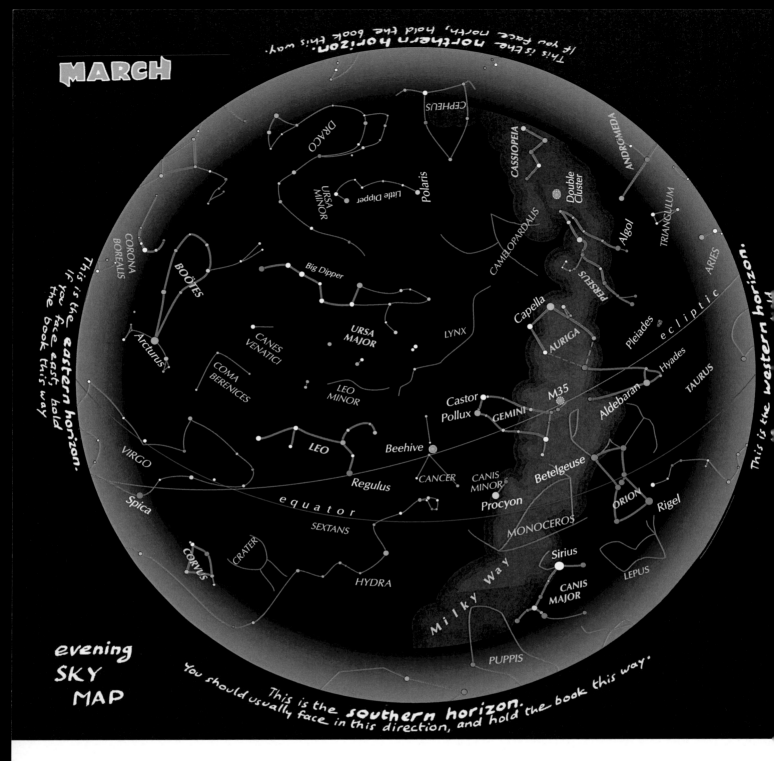

MARCH

CEPHEUS

DRACO

URSA MINOR

Little Dipper

Polaris

CASSIOPEIA

Double Cluster

ANDROMEDA

Algol

TRIANGULUM

ARIES

CAMELOPARDALIS

PERSEUS

CORONA BOREALIS

BOÖTES

Big Dipper

LYNX

Capella

AURIGA

ecliptic

Pleiades

Arcturus

CANES VENATICI

URSA MAJOR

Hyades

TAURUS

COMA BERENICES

LEO MINOR

M35

Aldebaran

Castor

Pollux

GEMINI

This is the eastern horizon.
If you face east, hold the book this way

VIRGO

LEO

Beehive

CANCER

CANIS MINOR

Betelgeuse

ORION

Rigel

This is the western horizon.

Regulus

Procyon

equator

Spica

SEXTANS

MONOCEROS

Sirius

LEPUS

CORVUS

CRATER

HYDRA

Milky Way

CANIS MAJOR

evening
SKY
MAP

PUPPIS

The Dark Trench

In January and February you got to know the six great winter constellations: Orion, Canis Major, Canis Minor, Taurus, Auriga, and Gemini. Each lies partly in the Milky Way and has one or more very bright stars. The Milky Way is where we see stars most thickly; and this applies to the brightest stars as well as the faint ones.

Now, as the year goes on, we are coming to the next region to the left (east), outside the Milky Way. The bright winter constellations are still in view on March evenings, but they have moved lower down toward the west.

When we now look at the middle of the sky we are looking at a region which is rather empty, a sort of black trench lying parallel to the Milky Way. There are stars, of course, but relatively few and faint ones. Out of these, people have had to form constellations.

Cancer, the Crab

Leftward (southeast) from Gemini is a constellation as well known as Gemini, even though it is one of the faintest of these faint constellations: Cancer. Why is it well known? We'll come to that shortly.

Cancer means "crab" in Latin. In the middle of Cancer is a cluster of faint stars. Two other stars stand north and south of the cluster. One leg extends from the northern star, and two from the southern. So the crab has only three legs instead of eight.

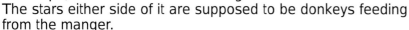

People have had many legends about the stars, and so the same stars may have various conflicting names. You would think that the cluster in the middle of Cancer would be called something like "the Crab's Shell." It has two commonly used names, but neither of them has to do with crabs: it is called the Beehive, and it is also called Praesepe, which is Latin for a "manger"! The stars either side of it are supposed to be donkeys feeding from the manger.

This Beehive or Praesepe cluster is the third star-cluster you have met (after the Pleiades and Hyades). It's farther away than they are, so you can't really see any of its stars separately. You can only see it at all if the air is clear, and then it looks like a faint glow. But in binoculars or telescope it is a beautiful sight: a soft mound of stars.

Silly little constellations

You will have realized by now that constellations are not equal. There are "rich" ones like Orion, and ones that have less than a fair share of stars, like Cancer. There are small ones like Canis Minor, and ones like Hydra that cover huge areas.

And there are old ones and young ones. All the constellations we have mentioned so far are ancient—meaning that they were talked about by the Greeks, and probably by the Babylonians and still earlier peoples. But there are spaces between them. And in more recent times people have invented constellations to fill these spaces.

Up left (northeast) from Auriga and Gemini there are two of these new constellations called Camelopardalis and Lynx. The first means "giraffe" in Latin. The lynx is a cat-like animal with very good eyesight. These constellations are marked on the sky map, but you needn't bother to learn them. Actually they are not so little: the Giraffe constellation is large, with a long neck reaching up near the Pole Star. But they are just spaces empty of bright stars. The man who invented the Lynx constellation admitted that you have to have a lynx's eyes to see its stars!

Hydra, the Water-Serpent

Down left again is another faint constellation, but a huge one—far the longest of all constellations. It is Hydra, the water-snake. (*Hydor* is Greek for "water.")

Hercules, the strong man of Greek legends, was once sent to kill the Hydra. It had a hundred heads, and every time he cut off one, two grew in its place! The situation was getting worse, till he thought of burning the stump of each head before it could grow again.

The Hydra in the sky has only one head: a group of five or six stars, quite easy to see, close underneath Cancer. This head is now in the middle of the sky, yet Hydra is so long that its tail has not yet come into view! So we will explore the rest of it next month.

Besides the head stars, there is another star in Hydra easy to see. It is down in the water-snake's throat, like a frog that the snake has swallowed. As it is the only fairly bright star in this whole region of the sky, it has the name Alfard, which means in Arabic "the lonely.

More about March ⟶

The ecliptic and the zodiac

We have mentioned the "ecliptic" already. What is this mysterious line?

It is the line in the sky along which the Sun moves. And the Moon and planets move along it too, though not so exactly. Sometimes people call it "the Road of the Sun."

You can see on the sky map that the ecliptic comes sloping out of the southeast side of Gemini and cuts through the very middle of Cancer. So this is the reason why Cancer is important. The moving bodies (Sun, Moon, planets) pass through it—whereas they never visit constellations far from the ecliptic such as Canis Major.

The constellations along the ecliptic are called "the zodiac." You have now visited three of them: Taurus, Gemini, and Cancer.

The equator of the sky

You know what the equator of the Earth is: an imaginary line around its middle, dividing it into two halves—the north hemisphere and the south. (*Hemisphere* means "half sphere.") Well, the equator of the sky (or celestial equator) is, likewise, an imaginary line dividing the sky into two equal hemispheres.

For instance, look at Orion, who is still in view. The celestial equator cuts across his middle. His arms and head are in the northern half of the sky, and from the waist down he is in the southern half.

Canis Major is completely in the southern hemisphere. From our position on the northern hemisphere of the Earth, we can see the northern hemisphere of the sky and also quite a lot of the southern.

The celestial equator is an imaginary line, but you can easily imagine where it is by using Orion's belt. The star at the upper, right-hand end of the belt is almost exactly on the equator. If you were to watch it for many hours, you would see it "drawing" the equator across the sky.

Spring

Toward the end of March comes a moment that you can call "the middle of spring." (In some years it is on March 20, in others March 21.) Some people call this moment "the beginning of spring." The safest way is to call it by its proper name, the spring equinox. What really happens at this time each year?

The Sun always travels along the line called the ecliptic. "Winter" is the time when the Sun is well down on the southern part of the ecliptic, because then it is lower down in the sky (for us who live in the northern hemisphere): It is shining more on the southern half of the Earth. What happens about March 21 is that the Sun comes to the place where the ecliptic crosses the celestial equator. It is now overhead on the Earth's equator, and shining equally on both halves of the Earth.

After this, it will move on along the ecliptic, into the northern half of the sky. It will be shining more on the northern half of the Earth, and we will have summer. Spring is the time between winter and summer.

Our sky map shows the sky about 9 o'clock. The Sun has set in the west, off the map to the right. You can draw the curves of the ecliptic and equator off the map to the place where they would cross. This is where the Sun is at the spring equinox.

Change clocks!

The *second Sunday in March* is the day to wind your clock one hour *forward*.

In winter, clocks are kept on Standard Time. This is about the same as the natural time that you can tell from the Sun. For instance, "mid-day" or "noon" is when the Sun is at its highest, in the south; well, 12 noon by Standard Time *is* when the Sun is highest.

But, though noon stays in its place in the middle of the day, sunrise does not stay at the same time. As we move from winter to summer, the Sun keeps rising earlier. In old times, everyone got up about dawn, whatever the clock said. Nowadays, everyone has to be at school or work by, say, 8 o'clock and so they get up about 7, however light or dark it is. In winter this works all right, but as sunrise gets earlier they find themselves getting up in bright sunlight and missing part of the day. That is why the lawmakers decided we should put our clocks an hour earlier in the summer, so that we are still getting up nearer to sunrise. They call this "Daylight-Saving Time."

It doesn't "save" any daylight, and is a stupid invention that makes many things confusing. It doesn't work for places farther north or south. Instead of changing clocks to the untrue time, it would be better to change the opening times of school or work in summer.

We go back from "Daylight-Saving Time" to Standard Time on the first Sunday in November. If it's hard to remember which way to twist the clock, say to yourself: "Spring forward, Fall back!"

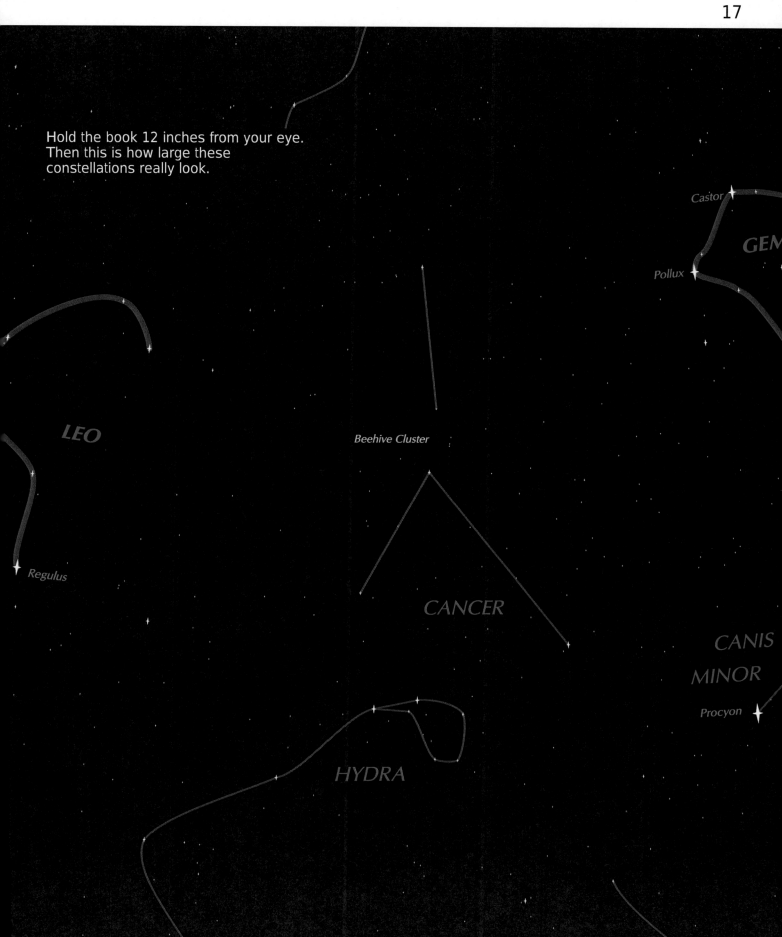

Hold the book 12 inches from your eye.
Then this is how large these
constellations really look.

Castor

GEM

Pollux

Beehive Cluster

LEO

Regulus

CANCER

CANIS

MINOR

Procyon

HYDRA

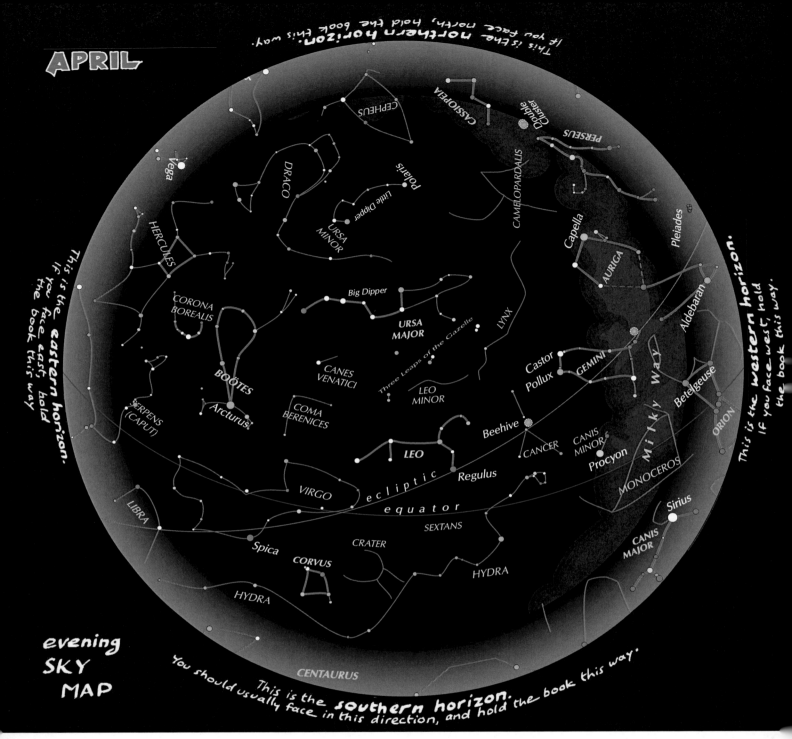

This is the eastern horizon. If you face east, hold the book this way

This is the western horizon. If you face west, hold the book this way.

You should usually face in this direction, and hold the book this way. This is the southern horizon.

evening
SKY
MAP

Leo, the Lion

After leaving the bright constellations of the Milky Way and crossing the "empty trench" of sky in which Cancer lies, we come to another bright constellation: Leo, the lion. It is one of the easiest constellations to recognize, because it really looks like a lion—or at least you can easily imagine it that way.

The bright star, Regulus, is the lion's heart. Above it is a C-shaped curve of stars: his mane and head. He faces to the right.

There is a considerable gap where his back should be, and then you come to a large triangle of fairly bright stars: they represent the end of his back, his back legs, and his tail. The tail star is the second brightest in the constellation after Regulus. It has a name, Denebola, from Arabic words meaning "tail of the lion."

Leo is another constellation of the zodiac: that is, the ecliptic passes through it. Regulus is very close to the ecliptic. so the

Moon and planets pass near it and sometimes even in front of it.

But if you have a telescope the most interesting star in Leo is the second one above Regulus, where the lion's back joins onto his mane. This star, called Algieba, is actually a double star.

Below Leo, the "empty trench" of sky continues, with the long, long Water-Snake constellation still winding along it. Above Leo and parallel with him is the Big Dipper.

Ursa Major, the Great Bear

The Big Dipper is now at its highest position in the sky. If you are still facing south, as we advised, you will have to tip your head way back to look at the Big Dipper. It will certainly be easiest if you are lying on your back, with your feet pointing south. At any rate keep looking at it with your chin southward and resist the temptation to turn around and face north! Next month we'll let you turn around and look at it the other way.

The Big Dipper is even better known than Orion and the Pleiades. There must be many people who know just this one group of stars. It has many other names. In England it is called the Plough (which is spelt "plow" in America). Other people call it Charles's Wain, or the Churl's Wain. (A *wain* was a wagon; a *churl* was a peasant.)

But its official name in astronomy is the Great Bear (in Latin, Ursa Major). This is strange, because a bear is one of the things it does *not* look like. Bears don't have tails!

Let us number the seven stars 1, 2, 3 . . . starting from the right or west. Numbers 1 to 4 make the square pan or bowl of the Dipper; numbers 4 to 7 make the handle. (Number 4 belongs to both bowl and handle, being the star where they join.) The seven stars also have names, but you don't have to learn them. For instance the joining-star, number 4, is called Megrez.

The shape does look like a dipper, or a plow. But it is a subtle shape. Draw a sketch of it from memory. Then look at the real thing, and you will probably find you got it wrong. A hint: the almost straight line through stars 6, 5, and 4 does *not* point at 1, but diagonally across the bowl to 2.

(See our sketch on the next page.)

Are the seven stars equally bright? (Look first, before reading the answers to these questions.) Answer: not quite. The faintest is number 4, Megrez. The brightest is number 5 next to it (which has the name Alioth).

Are the seven all the same color? No: number 1 (Dubhe) is noticeably more orange than the others. Also number 7 at the other end (Alkaid) is slightly bluer, but this is harder to see.

Are the seven stars really a cluster of stars close together in space, or are some of them much farther away than others? This of course is not something you can see; it can only be found out by scientific studies. The answer is that the five of the same color *are* a real cluster in space. In fact it is the nearest star-cluster to us, nearer than the Hyades, Pleiades, and Beehive, which is why it appears so large and spread-out. The two end stars, 1 and 7, are a bit farther away and do not belong to the cluster.

The stolen sister

Which of the seven has a faint companion star close to it? Be sure to look for yourself first. This is a test of eyesight.

Answer: number 6 (called Mizar), at the bend of the Dipper's handle. The little star close to it, on the outer side of the bend, is called Alcor. Mizar and Alcor are a "double star," like Algieba in Leo. They are a very wide-apart pair: most others are much closer together, so that it's only in a telescope that you can see the two stars separately.

So the seven stars of the Big Dipper are really eight—which reminds us that the Seven Sisters (the Pleiades) are, to most people, only six. The Mongol people of central Asia have a story that explains both. The Seven Brothers went in search of a wife, and stole away one of the Seven Sisters. So there is the Lost Pleiad in a different part of the sky— Alcor!

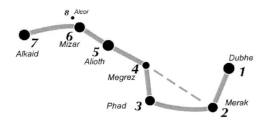

Here's what your sketch of the Big Dipper should look like. We've added the 8th star: Alcor.

Canes Venatici, the Hunting Dogs

Under the bear's tail, two little dogs are snapping at him. So there are three dog constellations in the sky, containing four dogs. But this is a "silly little constellation," invented not long ago. There are only two noticeable stars. The brighter of them has the name Cor Caroli, which means in Latin "heart of Charles." It was named for King Charles I or King Charles II of England—nobody is sure which.

Join the dots

Here are the stars of six constellations that you should remember. (You met them a few months ago and they're gradually disappearing now.) See if you can draw the lines between them—or even the pictures around them!

More of Ursa Major

The Big Dipper is only part of Ursa Major. There is a large area to the right and below (west and south) which also belongs to this constellation. If we really try to draw a Bear, the Dipper is only his back and tail. (But bears don't have tails!)

Along the southern edge of Ursa Major's area are three pairs of stars. We could see them as three of the bear's feet (the fourth being hidden). But the traditional name they have is different: the Three Leaps of the Gazelle. The Arabs didn't know of bears, but they knew gazelles, those beautiful deer-like animals of the desert. They imagined a gazelle bounding through this part of the sky, leaving three pairs of hoof-prints.

The Lyrid meteors

On April 21 (or 22 in some years) comes another of those times when we expect to see more meteors than usual. If you would like to watch for them, first read about meteor showers on page 72.

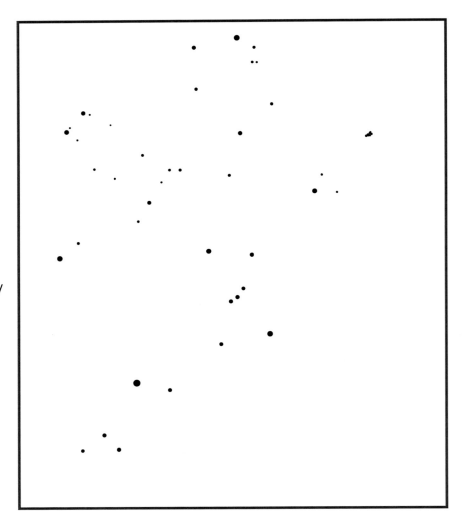

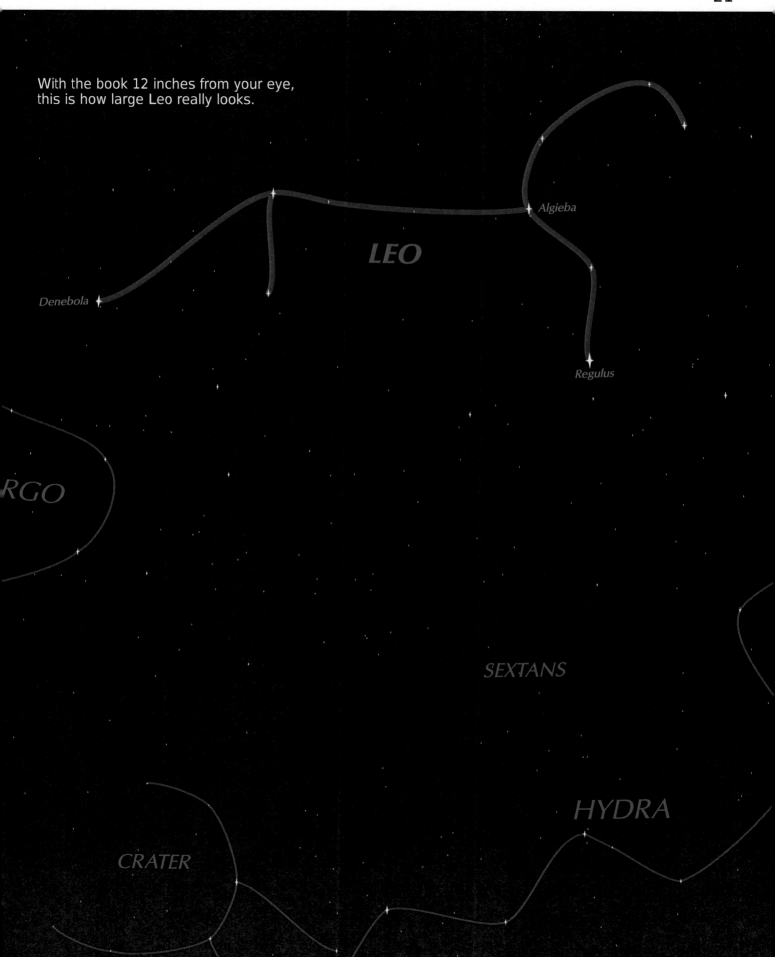

With the book 12 inches from your eye,
this is how large Leo really looks.

LEO

Algieba

Denebola

Regulus

RGO

SEXTANS

HYDRA

CRATER

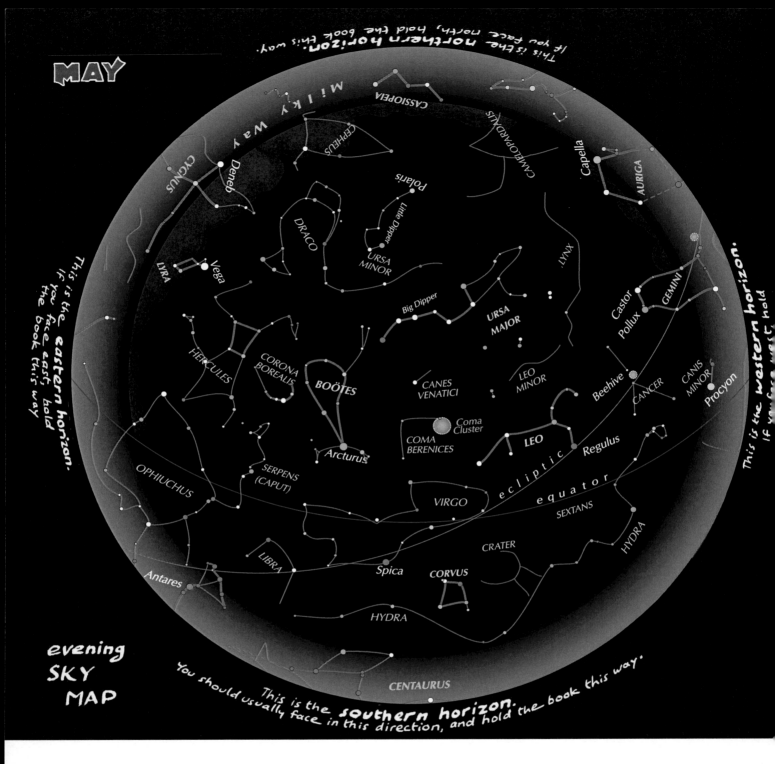

MAY

CASSIOPEIA

CEPHEUS

CAMELOPARDALIS

Capella

AURIGA

Polaris

Little Dipper

DRACO

URSA
MINOR

LYNX

CYGNUS

Deneb

MILKY WAY

Castor

GEMINI

Pollux

Vega

LYRA

Big Dipper

URSA
MAJOR

Beehive

CANCER

CANIS
MINOR

Procyon

HERCULES

CORONA
BOREALIS

BOÖTES

CANES
VENATICI

LEO
MINOR

Coma
Cluster

COMA
BERENICES

LEO

Regulus

Arcturus

ecliptic

This is the **eastern horizon.**
If you face east, hold
the book this way

OPHIUCHUS

SERPENS
(CAPUT)

VIRGO

equator

SEXTANS

CRATER

HYDRA

Antares

LIBRA

Spica

CORVUS

HYDRA

**evening
SKY
MAP**

CENTAURUS

The bare spring sky

To the left of Leo we are in another empty-looking area. In fact the whole sky in May has an empty look, in spite of Leo and the Big Dipper. There is a reason for this.

The largest numbers of stars are in or near the Milky Way. This is true of bright stars as well as faint stars. The Milky Way is now lying nearly flat around the horizon. In the sky map you can see most of the circle of the Milky Way. (It is tilted slightly: you can see the northernmost part of it in Cassiopeia, but the southernmost part is still too low to see, below the southern horizon.) But in the real sky you probably can't see any of it: near the horizon there is too much haze, light, and obstruction. The area overhead is as far as possible from the Milky Way and has the fewest bright stars, though of course it does have some.

The Milky Way is really a huge "pancake" of stars. On May evenings the pancake is lying flat. Really, it is the Earth that has turned to a position where you are looking straight out of the pancake. So there are fewest stars above you.

Around the Pole

Since last month the Big Dipper has swung to the west and begun to slope downward. This is part of the same turning-motion that makes Orion, Leo and all the constellations roll over toward the west. When they reach the horizon they "set"—that is, disappear from our view.

But the Big Dipper is too far north to do this. Instead it will move in a circle around the Pole Star. At its lowest (which will be about October—see the sky map for then) it will be down near the horizon, but still above it.

The same applies to the other constellations that you can see on the map near Ursa Major: Draco, Ursa Minor, Cepheus, and Cassiopeia. We call them the "circumpolar" constellations, which just means "around the Pole."

This is getting awkward to look at! If you are still lying on your back with your feet southward, your chin is now tilted right back, to look at the Big Dipper, which is farther *back* than overhead. You have gotten used to seeing the middle-of-the-sky constellations like Orion and Leo pass across in front of you like a procession, from left to right. Remember this and don't get confused! Now we will let you get up and turn around, to face north, for a special look at the constellations around the Pole. Turn the book around too, so that the words "northern horizon" (beside the map) are the right way up, because the real northern horizon is in front of you.

The circumpolar constellations never set. They keep circling around the Pole, like pictures drawn on a huge clock. But this clock turns in the wrong or "counter-clockwise" direction. The stars now seem to be rolling from right to left. That is because *you* have turned around!

The nearer a star is to the Pole, the smaller the circle it moves in, and the slower it moves. That makes sense, doesn't it? If you put a spot of paint half way along the hand of a clock, it will move more slowly than the tip of the hand and make a smaller circle, though they both go around in the same time.

The Pole Star

Finally, there is one bright star so near the middle of the "clock" that it makes only a tiny circle. People usually say it doesn't move at all. This isn't quite true, but for most purposes it is true enough.

The still point in the turning sky is the North Celestial Pole (that means, the north pole of the sky). And the star that marks it is the Pole Star. You can also call it the North Star, or the North Pole Star, or Polaris (which is "polar" in Latin).

It is useful because it shows where north is. North in the sky means any direction leading toward the Pole Star. On the Earth you cannot, of course, climb up in the sky toward the Pole Star. But if you walk toward the place on the horizon under the Pole Star, you will be walking north. If you go far enough in that direction, you will reach the North Pole (of the Earth).

So it is useful to be able to identify the Pole Star in the sky. You'd better learn this: as soon as your friends hear you are interested in astronomy, they are liable to say "All right, show me the Pole Star!"

Now your knowledge of the Big Dipper comes in handy. Stars 1 and 2 of the Dipper (the two that make the end of the bowl) are called Dubhe and Merak. They are also called "The Pointers to the Pole." They point roughly to the Pole Star. The distance from Dubhe to the Pole Star is about 5 times the distance between Dubhe and Merak.

Coma Berenices, the Hair of Berenice

Remember that Leo the lion ends at the star Denebola, which is supposed to be his tail? Well, in ancient times he had a longer tail, ending in a tuft. This is the fuzzy cluster of stars up to the left from Denebola. You may not be able to see this cluster if the sky is not clear. Look for it with binoculars.

There is a story about Queen Berenice of Egypt, who lived more than two thousand years ago and had long golden hair. Her husband, King Ptolemy III, went away to fight a war because his sister was in danger, and Berenice promised the gods that if he returned safely she would make a sacrifice of her hair. He did return safely, so Berenice cut off her hair and hung it up in a temple. But the hair was so beautiful that somebody stole it. The king

was furious, and threatened to punish the priests of the temple for their carelessness. A quick-witted astronomer called Conon happened to be standing by. He pointed up at this cluster of stars and said: "Behold! The gods have placed Her Majesty's hair in the sky!" The king believed him; evidently he had never noticed these stars before. So everyone was happy—the king, the priests, the thief—except perhaps Leo, who had lost the tuft of his tail!

So this small part of the sky, with the cluster in it, became known as a new constellation, called Coma Berenices, "Berenice's Hair." It is still one of the official constellations, unlike some more recently invented ones that have been dropped.

Apart from the fuzzy cluster, there are only about three noticeable stars in the constellation.

The Realm of Galaxies

But far beyond these stars and the Coma cluster, there are in this part of the sky many galaxies. (To see them you need to use a telescope.) They spread south into Virgo, and north into Ursa Major. So this area of the sky is interesting, even though there are few bright stars in it. It has been called the Realm of Galaxies.

You can understand that when we look straight outward from our own galaxy—our pancake of stars—we can most easily see other galaxies. Galaxies that lie in the same direction as the Milky Way are hidden by the foreground stars in our own galaxy.

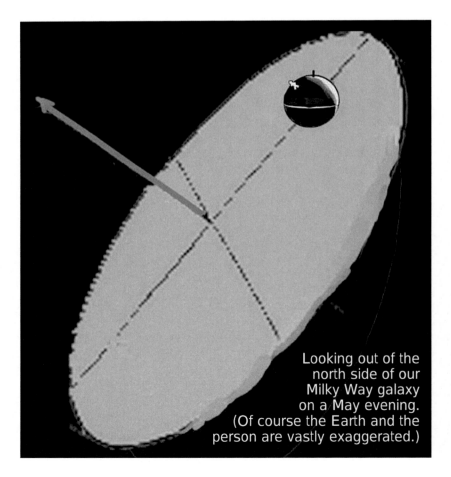

Looking out of the north side of our Milky Way galaxy on a May evening. (Of course the Earth and the person are vastly exaggerated.)

The Eta Aquarid meteors

This is another meteor shower, which you can see about May 4 each year. It has an interesting connection with the famous Halley's Comet. If you think of watching it, read first about meteor showers on page 73. Warning: to see the Eta Aquarids it is necessary to be up well after midnight or else get up early in the morning.

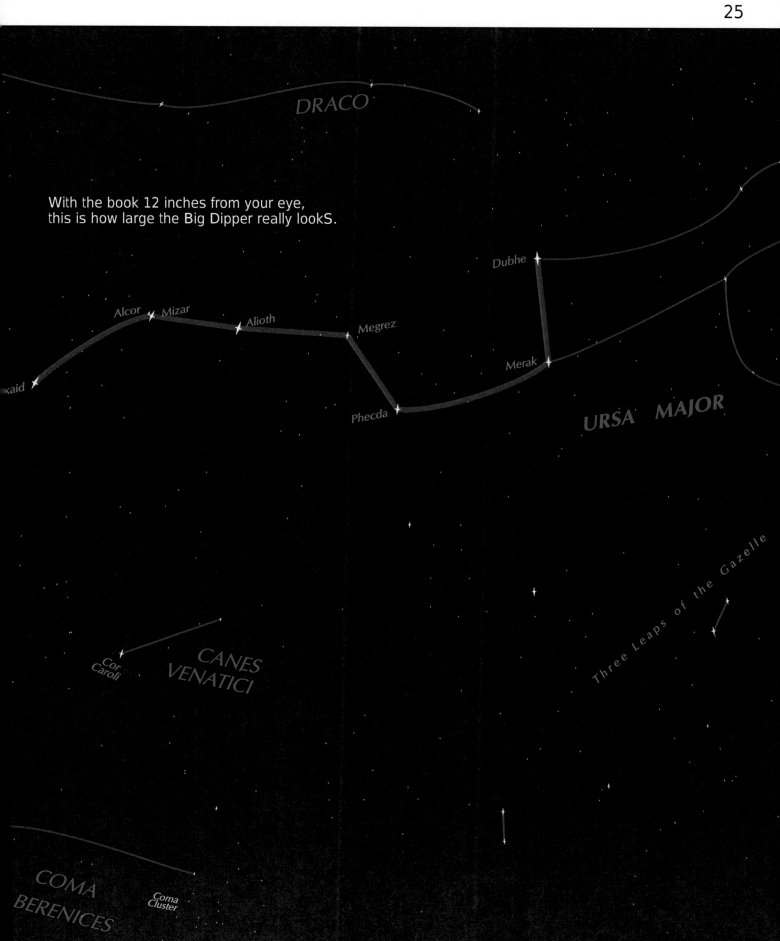

With the book 12 inches from your eye,
this is how large the Big Dipper really lookS.

DRACO

Dubhe

Alcor Mizar Alioth Megrez

Merak

Phecda

URSA MAJOR

xaid

CANES
VENATICI

Cor
Caroli

Three Leaps of the Gazelle

COMA
BERENICES

Coma
Cluster

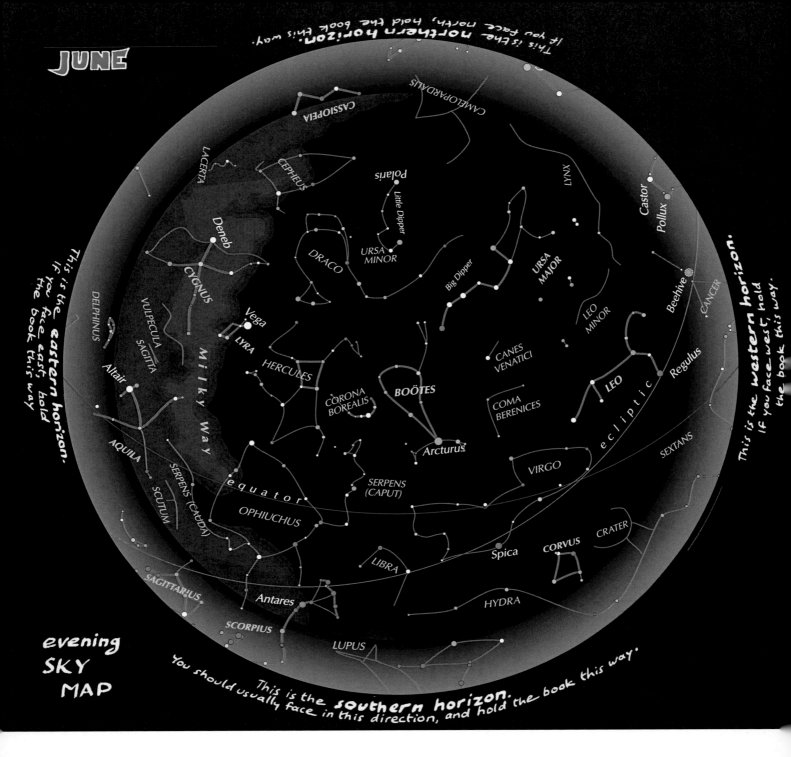

This is the **northern horizon.**
If you face north, hold the book this way.

CAMELOPARDALIS

CASSIOPEIA

LACERTA

CEPHEUS

Polaris

Little Dipper

URSA MINOR

DRACO

LYNX

Deneb

CYGNUS

Vega

LYRA

HERCULES

Big Dipper

URSA MAJOR

Castor

Pollux

VULPECULA

SAGITTA

DELPHINUS

Milky Way

Beehive

CANCER

LEO MINOR

CANES VENATICI

CORONA BOREALIS

BOÖTES

COMA BERENICES

LEO

Regulus

Altair

AQUILA

SCUTUM

SERPENS (CAUDA)

equator

OPHIUCHUS

SERPENS (CAPUT)

Arcturus

VIRGO

ecliptic

SEXTANS

SAGITTARIUS

Antares

LIBRA

Spica

CORVUS

CRATER

SCORPIUS

HYDRA

LUPUS

This is the **eastern horizon.** If you face east, hold the book this way

This is the **western horizon.** If you face west, hold the book this way.

This is the **southern horizon.** You should usually face in this direction, and hold the book this way.

evening SKY MAP

Boötes, the Herdsman

The rather empty sky of spring and early summer evenings has one very bright star in the middle: Arcturus. It is almost overhead now. You can be sure you are looking at it when you notice its slightly golden color.

As if it wasn't easy enough to find, there is another way of finding it. Look at the Big Dipper. Its handle is bent. Imagine this curve continuing on south, quite a long way, and it will lead you to Arcturus.

Arcturus is about 40 light-years away. In 1933 a big exhibition was held at Chicago. Light from Arcturus was used to switch on the illuminations, because this light had left the star at the time of a Chicago exhibition 40 years before.

Arcturus is the chief star of Boötes. In fact it is the only very bright star in the constellation.

The dots over the second *o* in *Boötes* mean that you pronounce the vowels separately: *oh-OH*, not *OO*. It is a Greek word meaning a man who tends a herd of cows, so we might call this the Cowboy constellation. If only it made a shape like a cowboy, or even his hat or *boots!*

Boötes does have a fairly clear shape: a balloon above Arcturus, two groups of three stars to left and right of Arcturus, and another group of three reaching toward the Big Dipper

Virgo, the Maiden

Make that curve from the Big Dipper's handle to Arcturus, and then continue it another long way southward: you will come to another lonely bright star. It is not quite so bright as Arcturus, and instead of being golden it is pure white. This star is Spica.

A saying that helps people to remember this is: "Make an arc to Arcturus, then drive a spike to Spica."

Arcturus is the chief star of Boötes, and Spica is the chief star of Virgo. They are the only really bright stars in their constellations; the rest are hard to see.

Virgo is an unmarried woman (it is the Latin word from which our *virgin* comes). You can make this picture out of the stars, but it is easier on paper than in the real sky! The constellation is large and dim. The girl is twice as large as the lion next to her!

Like Leo, Virgo is important because the Sun, Moon and planets pass through it. In other words, it is another of the zodiacal constellations, along the ecliptic. Spica is close to the actual ecliptic, though not so close as Regulus in Leo.

Spica means in Latin an "ear" of wheat, that is, the seed-head of the wheat plant, from which we make bread. The girl, according to one story, is holding this in her hand because she is Proserpina, daughter of Ceres the goddess of the *cereals* and other plants. Pluto, the god of death, saw Proserpina in the fields and stole her away to the underworld to be his wife. While her mother went wandering sadly in search of her, nothing would grow. At last Pluto had to let Proserpina live in the upper world for half of each year; and this is summer, when Ceres is happy and the crops will grow.

So Proserpina's picture is in the sky in summer. The equator runs through it, so it is half in the north of the sky and half in the south, rather like Proserpina spending half her time above ground and half below.

In the Bible is the story of Ruth, a poor girl who lived by gleaning in the field of a farmer called Boaz. That is, she followed behind the harvesters and picked up the scraps of wheat they dropped. Boaz fell in love with her and married her. An astronomer in the seventeenth century wanted us to use Biblical names in the sky instead of "pagan" ones, so he made the rather good suggestion that Virgo, gleaning wheat, should be Ruth, and Boötes, standing above her, should be Boaz.

More of Hydra; and three little constellations on its back

Below Virgo, the ridiculously long constellation Hydra is still continuing. It runs all the way under the zodiacal constellations Cancer, Leo, and Virgo. This watersnake now lies around a quarter of the horizon, from the west to the south. But it will be hard to see in the horizon hazes. Anyway there is no clear line of stars: the stars chosen to be part of Hydra are far apart.

To make it more difficult, there are three "silly little constellations" close above Hydra, between it and the ecliptic.

Actually only the first of these is of the "silly" kind, invented in modern times. It is called Sextans (a sextant, an instrument for measuring positions of stars) and is under Leo.

Next is Crater, which means a cup. Its stars, too, are faint; but they do make a shape like a tilted cup, and the constellation was an ancient one.

The third small constellation is Corvus, the crow. It is easy to see: six quite bright stars close together in a symmetrical shape which you can make into a bird. Yet surprisingly few people have even heard of Corvus.

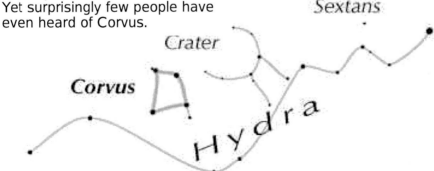

Ursa Minor, the Little Bear

You have already learnt the Pole Star, and how to find it by using the two pointer stars in the Big Dipper.

It has a separate constellation to be in: Ursa Minor. You could call it Ursula, a girl's name that means "Little Bear"!

Just as the seven chief stars in Ursa Major are also called the Big Dipper, so the seven stars of Ursa Minor are also called the Little Dipper.

One difference is the shape of the dipper. Its handle curves the opposite way.

Another difference is the brightness of the stars. Only two of them are at all bright: the Pole Star at one end, and a star at the opposite end, called Kokab. This simply means "star" in the Arabic and Hebrew languages.

When you are trying to find the Pole Star, Kokab is the star you might confuse with it. In the region above the Big Dipper's bowl, there are just these two noticeable stars. Ways to tell which is which are: the two Pointers point to the Pole Star; and Kokab is slightly orange.

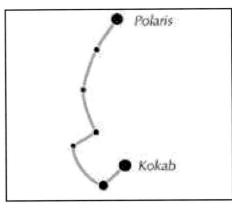

The other stars in the Little Dipper are faint. Their only importance is that they are in the Pole Star's constellation: they are needed to make a Dipper! If it were not for the Pole Star, people might not have bothered to make a constellation here.

Another difference from Ursa Major is that there are no other parts to the constellation. This line of seven stars is all. In June the line points straight up from the Pole toward the zenith, or part of the sky over your head.

If the Little Dipper is to become a bear, the pan must be all of the bear's body, and the handle is proportionately a much longer tail. The story has to be that the bear had a stumpy tail, which was pinned to the Pole, and the whirling motion around the Pole has stretched it. But this cannot explain Ursa Major's tail, which droops away from the Pole.

There must be **some** reason why mankind associates bears—presumably polar bears—with these constellations. When Europeans landed in North America, they found that some of the Indian tribes also call Ursa Major a bear.

Midsummer

June 21 (or, in some years, 20) is what is called the *summer solstice*. Each day, the Sun has been traveling a little higher across the sky, and the days were getting gradually longer. Now the Sun reaches its highest, and there is the longest time of daylight. After this the Sun will start to be a little lower in the sky each day, and the days will get shorter.

This may seem surprising, because the weather goes on getting hotter for a month or two after this. The Sun has been heating the land; it takes a while for the land to cool down.

On the sky map, follow the line of the ecliptic to the western edge. The Sun is always on the ecliptic, moving slowly east. It is now between the constellations Taurus and Gemini. You can figure out where this is; it is off to the right of this month's sky map, because the sky map shows the time a few hours after the Sun has set. You can also figure out that this is the part of the ecliptic highest north of the other line, the equator. This is why the Sun at this time of year spends longest in the sky, and passes highest above our heads.

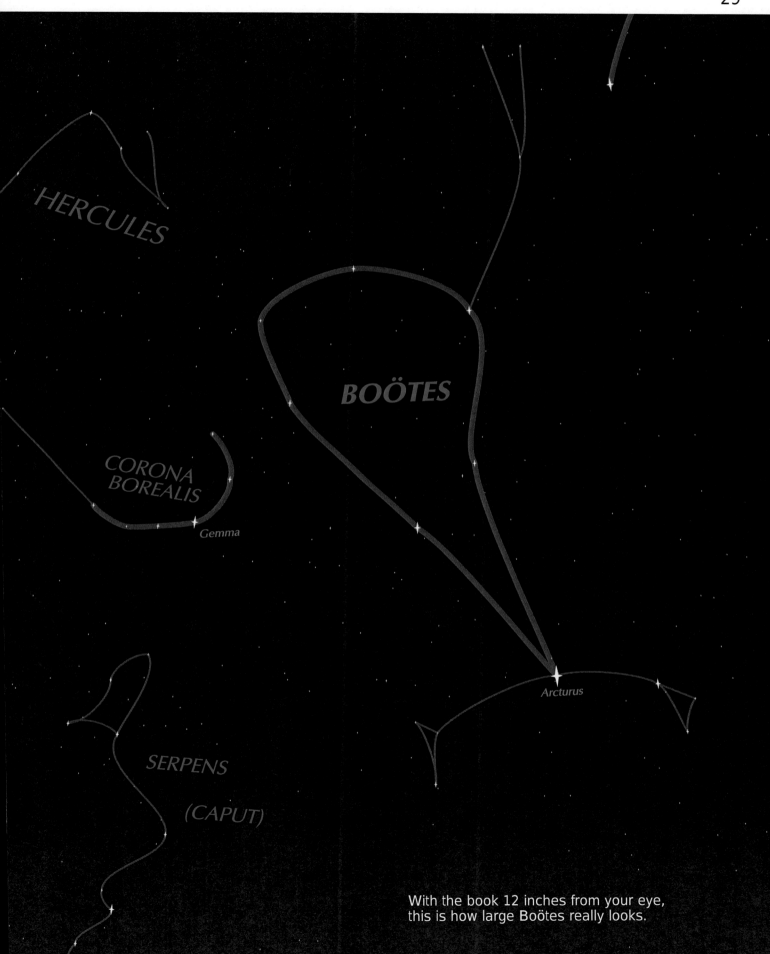

HERCULES

BOÖTES

CORONA BOREALIS

Gemma

SERPENS

(CAPUT)

Arcturus

With the book 12 inches from your eye,
this is how large Boötes really looks.

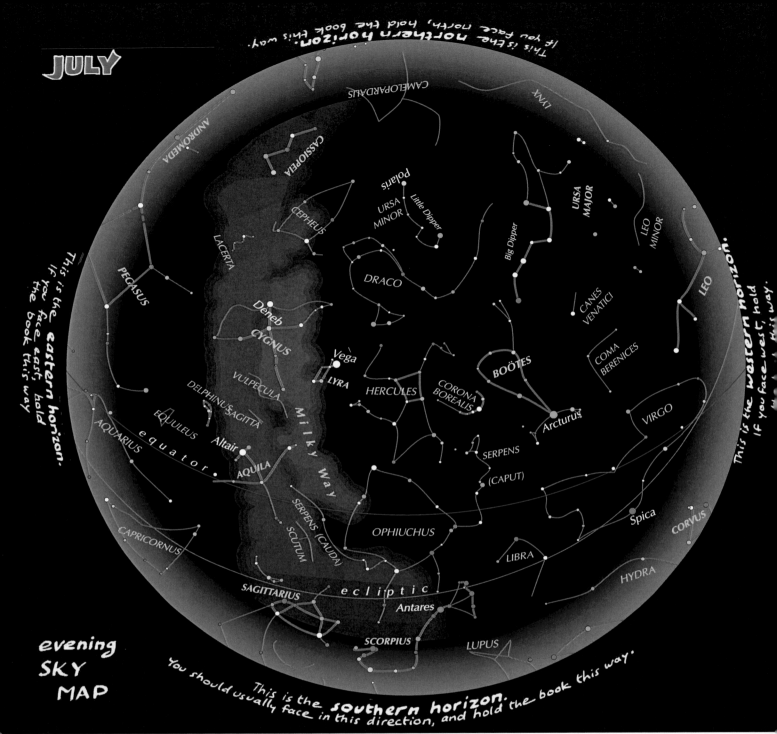

This is the **northern horizon.** If you face north, hold the book this way.

JULY

CAMELOPARDALIS

LYNX

ANDROMEDA

CASSIOPEIA

CEPHEUS

Polaris

URSA MINOR

Little Dipper

URSA MAJOR

Big Dipper

LEO MINOR

LACERTA

DRACO

LEO

PEGASUS

CANES VENATICI

Deneb

CYGNUS

VULPECULA

Vega

LYRA

BOÖTES

COMA BERENICES

DELPHINUS SAGITTA

HERCULES

CORONA BOREALIS

Arcturus

VIRGO

EQUULEUS

Altair

e q u a t o r

AQUILA

SERPENS

Spica

AQUARIUS

(CAPUT)

CORVUS

M i l k y   W a y

SERPENS (CAUDA)

SCUTUM

OPHIUCHUS

LIBRA

HYDRA

CAPRICORNUS

SAGITTARIUS

e c l i p t i c

Antares

LUPUS

SCORPIUS

This is the **eastern horizon.** If you face east, hold the book this way.

This is the **western horizon.** If you face west, hold the book this way.

evening SKY MAP

You should usually face in this direction, and hold the book this way. This is the **southern horizon.**

The summer Milky Way

The Milky Way is climbing higher in the sky again, as it was in the middle of winter. But this is a different part of it. In fact this part is in the opposite direction in space.

In the winter sky, there are many very bright stars, such as those of Orion, but the Milky Way is quite thin and pale. In the summer sky it is the other way around: the impressive part is not the single bright stars (though there are a few) but the background of the Milky Way itself. It is brighter, with especially dense patches— "star clouds." And it swells to its widest at the bottom of our sky map. This is called the "Central Bulge" of the Milky Way. When we look at it we are in fact looking toward the very center of our galaxy.

Libra, the Scales

Before reaching the summer Milky Way, we have to cross another dark area with few stars. I'm talking about us moving our eyes across the sky, but we could be talking about a planet or the Moon, moving along the ecliptic from Virgo through the bare area, which is called Libra.

Libra is the only star-picture in the zodiac that is not a person or animal. It is a balance, consisting of a beam with two pans hanging from it, for weighing things. The right-hand pan is tilted down, so the load must be heavier on that side.

Scorpius (or Scorpio)

Leaving Libra, we enter the bulge of the Milky Way through a line of six stars. These seem to me like a fence; planets coming along the ecliptic have to open a gate in it to get into the garden of the Milky Way. But, since this is the beginning of the Scorpion constellation, we are supposed to think of these stars as the front of the animal's face.

Scorpions have two large claws reaching forward. What happened to this scorpion's claws? They were cut off to form Libra. The Romans decided there should be separate constellations of the zodiac here; so they made the two claws of Scorpius into the arms of the balance, Libra.

This front part of the Scorpion began to come into view in May or June evenings. Now, as the whole figure rears up into the sky, it is a magnificent sight. It really looks like a huge scorpion, with long stinging tail curled over its back.

The bright star, Antares, is the scorpion's heart. It is flanked by a star on each side. Antares is one of the reddest stars. Its name means that it is the "rival of Mars." (In Greek *anti* means "against"; *Ares* was the god of war, whom the Romans called Mars.) The planet Mars is also reddish; when it goes along the ecliptic just north of Antares, they look as if they are trying to out-red each other. They are red for

different reasons: little Mars because it has reddish dust on its surface; huge Antares, millions of times farther away, because it is a star of the kind called "red giant" (like Betelgeuse).

Scorpius is the southernmost of the constellations we're going to visit. It is so far south in the sky that evenings near midsummer are about the only evenings to see it. Scorpions live in the deserts of hot countries like Mexico and Libya, so it is appropriate that the Scorpion constellation is well south in the sky and is seen in hot weather.

Remember how Orion (the first constellation you learned in January) was killed by the scorpion. Now the Orion in the sky keeps as far as he can from the scorpion in the sky. As soon as Orion sees Scorpius rising in the east, he sets in the west. They are, in fact, on opposite sides of the sky. Right now, when Scorpius is above the southern horizon, Orion is below the northern horizon.

Just as Orion is the brilliant central constellation of the winter evening sky, so Scorpius is the brilliant central constellation of the summer evening sky.

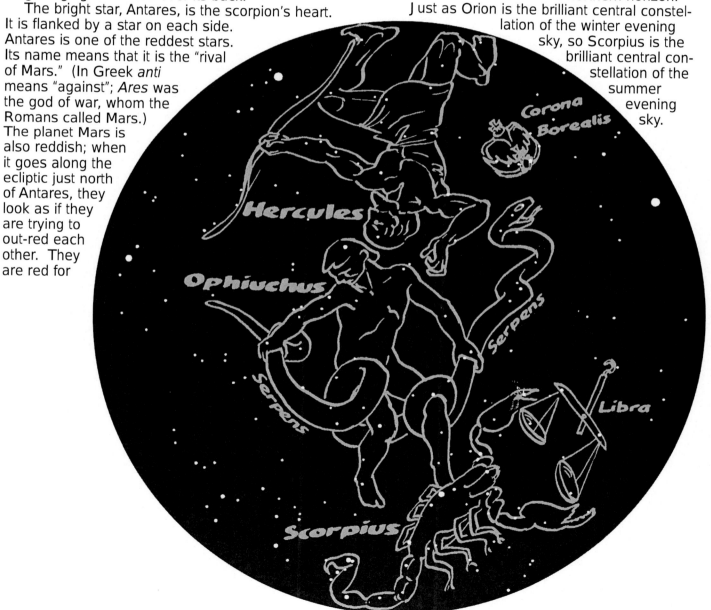

The Snake, the Snake-Holder, and more ⟶

Ophiuchus

Above Scorpius is a large man who leads a dangerous life. His name is Ophiuchus, which means "snake-holder" in Greek. Not only is he standing with one foot over the scorpion's head and one foot over the scorpion's stinger, but he is holding a snake in his hands.

The brightest star in Ophiuchus is at the top, called Rasalhague, which is from Arabic words meaning "head of the snake-man." The rest is a very wide space surrounded by a vague ring of stars, so he looks more like a balloon than a man.

You remember that the constellations through which the ecliptic passes are called the zodiac. Traditionally they are 12, and many people know the 12 names without really knowing what they are: Pisces, Aries, Taurus, Gemini, Cancer, Leo, Virgo, Libra, Scorpius, Sagittarius, Capricornus, Aquarius. But the ecliptic actually passes through the feet of Ophiuchus too. So Ophiuchus ought to be counted as a 13th zodiacal constellation. The Sun, Moon, and planets visit it. In fact they spend a longer time in it than in Scorpius, most of which is too far south.

Serpens, Head and Tail

The snake that Ophiuchus is holding forms another constellation, Serpens. (The Greek word for "snake" is *ophis*, the Latin is *serpens*, and in English too *serpent* is another word for "snake.")

Serpens is a strange constellation: the only one that is in two separate parts. They're called Serpens Cauda (on the left or east side of Ophiuchus) and Serpens Caput (on the right); Cauda is Latin for "tail" and Caput is "head." Perhaps Ophiuchus has torn the snake in two.

Whereas Ophiuchus is a mostly bare area, the Serpent's Tail lies along the Milky Way.

Hercules

Above Ophiuchus is another gigantic man of the sky: Hercules. He was the strongest man who ever lived, hero of countless Greek stories. One of them was about how he killed the Hydra, and perhaps that is why the Hydra constellation is now setting—only its tail can still be seen as it hurries out of sight!

Hercules is not easy to see. The stars are supposed to outline a man kneeling, and shooting an arrow. He is *upside down*. His head is a star that is nearer to Rasalhague in Ophiuchus than it is to the other stars in Hercules. It is called Rasalgethi, which means in Arabic "head of the kneeler."

The body of Hercules is formed by six stars, with a narrow waist. There is another name for the four northern stars (the waist and hips): the Keystone. A keystone is the stone at the top of an arch, and has this shape, narrower at one end. On a July evening these stars are at the zenith. If an arch were built across the sky, the keystone *would* be here.

A famous object is between the two back or western stars in the Keystone. It is the Great Globular Cluster in Hercules. In a small telescope it looks like a fuzzy patch; in large telescopes it looks like a snowball made of thousands of stars! There are many globular clusters in other parts of the sky, but this is one of the best. Clusters of this kind are much bigger, and much farther away, than clusters like the Pleiades, Hyades, Beehive, Big Dipper, and Coma Berenices.

The zenith

This word means the spot *overhead*; the direction *straight up* from you. It is the middle of the sky. It is the easiest place to observe if you are lying down, and the hardest if you are not!

The part of the sky that goes over your head depends on where you are on the Earth. If you live on the equator, the stars on the equator of the sky go over you. If you live at the north pole, then the Pole Star is always at your zenith. If you live about half way between (in North America or Europe), then constellations like Auriga, Boötes and Hercules pass above you.

Corona Borealis, the Northern Crown

Here is an easy, beautiful little constellation. It is between the two men, Boötes and Hercules, but nearer to Boötes. It is a semicircle of stars. In the middle is the brightest, Gemma, which means "jewel."

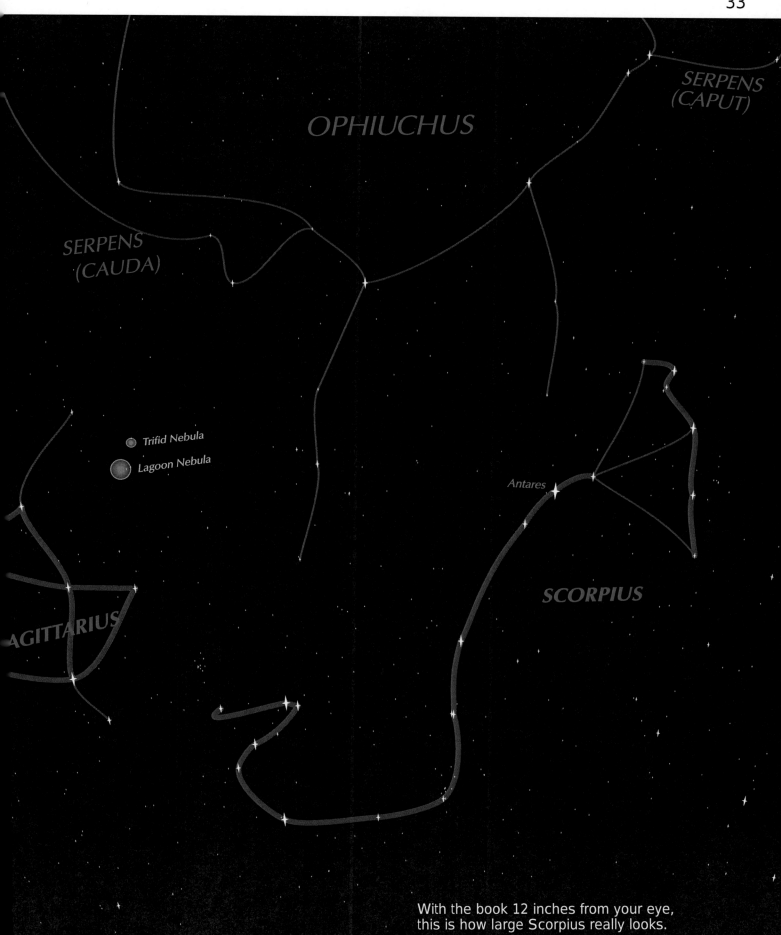

SERPENS
(CAPUT)

OPHIUCHUS

SERPENS
(CAUDA)

Trifid Nebula

Lagoon Nebula

Antares

SCORPIUS

AGITTARIUS

With the book 12 inches from your eye,
this is how large Scorpius really looks.

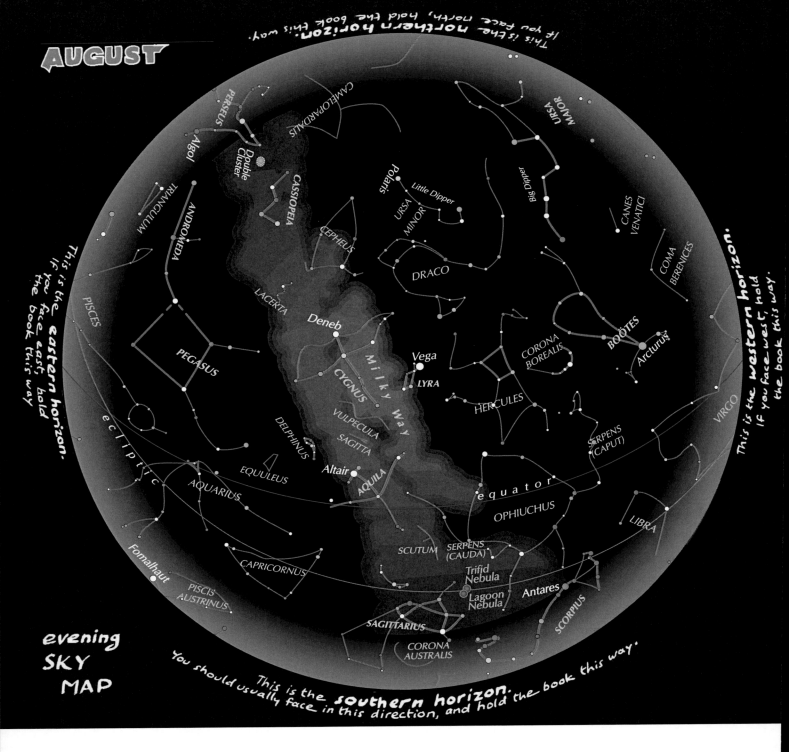

AUGUST

URSA MAJOR

PERSEUS

Algol

CAMELOPARDALIS

CANES VENATICI

Double Cluster

CASSIOPEIA

Polaris

Big Dipper

COMA BERENICES

TRIANGULUM

CEPHEUS

URSA MINOR

Little Dipper

ANDROMEDA

DRACO

BOÖTES

Arcturus

PISCES

LACERTA

Deneb

CORONA BOREALIS

This is the **eastern horizon**.
If you face east, hold the book this way

Milky Way

Vega

This is the **western horizon**.
If you face west, hold the book this way.

PEGASUS

CYGNUS

LYRA

HERCULES

VULPECULA

ecliptic

DELPHINUS

SAGITTA

SERPENS (CAPUT)

EQUULEUS

Altair

AQUILA

VIRGO

AQUARIUS

equator

OPHIUCHUS

LIBRA

SCUTUM

SERPENS (CAUDA)

CAPRICORNUS

Trifid Nebula

Fomalhaut

Lagoon Nebula

Antares

PISCIS AUSTRINUS

SAGITTARIUS

SCORPIUS

**evening
SKY
MAP**

CORONA AUSTRALIS

Sagittarius, the Archer

The "central bulge" of the Milky Way is shared between the two bright constellations Scorpius and Sagittarius, and the vaguer constellation Ophiuchus which ought to count as part of the zodiac too.

Sagittarius is a group of stars you will notice easily, though there is no one star as bright as Antares, and the stars do not make as clear a picture as the scorpion. Most people see the shape of a Teapot pouring tea onto the scorpion's tail.

The brightest star, at the top of the handle, is called Nunki.

But the ancient people saw an Archer: a man drawing a bow and arrow. In Latin, *sagitta* means "arrow." The bow is a good enough bow, if you remember that ancient bows were shaped like this

not this

There is not much of the man. He looks more like a butterfly. Moreover, he is supposed to be not just a man but a centaur. A centaur was a mythical beast, half man and half horse. The large mostly starless area left and downward from the bright stars in Sagittarius is also part of the constellation, so we have to imagine the body of the horse here.

The Archer is supposed to be shooting his arrow at the scorpion's heart (Antares), but his aim is low. Near the tip of the arrow, or of the teapot's spout, is the point that is thought to be the actual center of our Milky Way Galaxy.

All this thick part of the Milky Way is spangled with clusters of stars, and nebulas (clouds of shining dust). Two famous ones, beautiful in a telescope, lie just down and right from the top star of Sagittarius's bow, either side of the ecliptic: they have lovely names—the Lagoon Nebula and the Trifid Nebula. ("Trifid" means "split into three parts.")

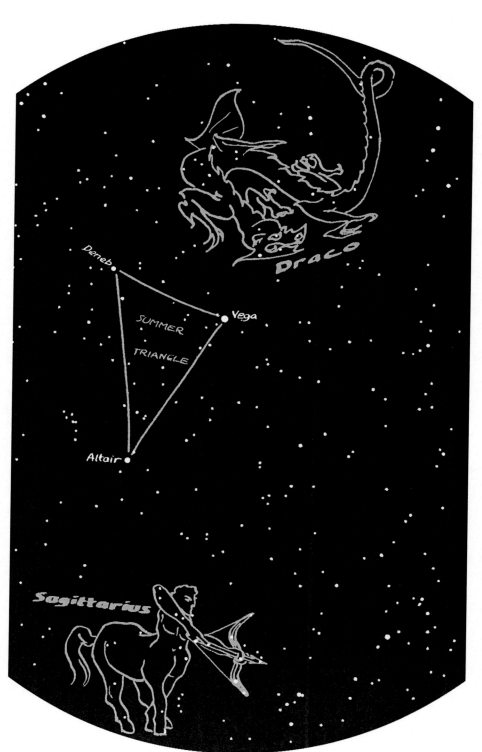

The dark rift

From here northward, the Milky Way seems to be split along the middle, like a sandwich. The darker the sky, the better you will be able to see the Milky Way, and the more sure you will feel that you are really seeing this dark band. What is the reason for it?

In the middle plane of the "pancake" of stars which is the Milky Way Galaxy, there are just as many or even more stars. But there is also a lot of dust. It is extremely rarefied compared with anything on Earth—that is, the particles of dust are far apart—but over huge distances it builds up like mist, and is enough to make the stars dimmer. So we see fewer stars. The dark lane is not really any kind of hole among the stars.

The Summer Triangle

High in the summer sky are three very bright stars, far apart: Deneb, Vega, and Altair.

Altair is the sharp point of the triangle, down near the equator. The other two are well north.

In the whole sky, Vega is the 5th brightest star; Altair is the 12th; Deneb is the 19th. Altair and Vega are stars a bit brighter than the Sun, and "only" 17 and 25 light-years away. But Deneb may be as much as *3,000* light-years away! Though it looks to us dimmer than Altair and Vega, it is actually one of the hugest and brightest stars known.

Draco, the Dragon

North of Vega and the feet of Hercules is a box of four or five stars. This is the head of Draco. The rest of the dragon constellation is a line of stars winding at first to the east, then back westward a long way, so that it goes all the way between the two Dippers (Ursa Major and Ursa Minor). It is not so ridiculously long as Hydra. But in a sense, since it is up near to the Pole, it wraps even farther around the sky: a third of the way around, from the Pointer Stars in the Big Dipper, as far as Vega and Deneb.

Late summer

June was the middle of summer, if you count that as being when the Sun was farthest north, the days longest and the nights shortest. Yet the weather usually goes on getting warmer for a while, so that July and August are the warmest months (for us in the northern hemisphere, that is). Why?

It's a delay-effect. The land and the sea go on getting heated by the Sun, and only later losing the heat.

The warm nights of August, which start a bit earlier than those of June and July, are pleasant for staying out and gazing at the stars. Overhead you see the Summer Triangle, very easy and impressive to point out to your friends! Below—in front of you—is the central part of the Milky Way, rich with star-clouds and clusters and nebulas. And, because of the Perseids, you have a good chance of seeing some "shooting stars."

The Dog Days

You may have heard of the Dog Days. These are the hot, sticky days that often come about August, when people and dogs get bad-tempered!

The dog that ancient people blamed for bringing this weather was the Dog Star—Sirius. How come, since we saw Sirius in the winter months of January and February, and it is now well below the horizon?

We are looking at the evening sky; if we were to wait till just before dawn, we would see Sirius appear before the Sun.

Each month, so far, we have been looking at the stars of evening—those that appear soon after darkness falls. To most of us, evening is the convenient time to look at stars, because our habit is to stay up late and get up late. So to us "the stars of August" are the stars of Sagittarius and its neighbors.

Since the weather is hot and school is out, why don't you try the experiment of getting up about 3 or 4 o'clock in the morning? You will be doing what farming people still do, and what ancient people mostly did. Go outside and you will see not the "August" sky but the sky we show in this book for November.

There is Orion, the great "winter" constellation, climbing into view! Remember that the three Belt stars of Orion point downward to Sirius? So, Sirius will rise in the next hour or so. By then the sky will be getting bright: the Sun will rise soon after Sirius. *This* is why, to ancient people, August was the time of the Dog Star.

Month names

July and August were named for Julius Caesar, who became the most powerful Roman, and his young relative Augustus, who became the first Roman emperor.

And the names of January, February, March, April, May and June all have stories behind them (for instance Janus, Mars, and Juno were Roman gods). But after August the months all have rather boring names that are just numbers: *septem, octo, novem, decem* are Latin for "seven, eight, nine, ten."

But September isn't the seventh month, it's the ninth!

What happened was that March was once the first month. Which made rather good sense: it's the month of spring.

The Perseid meteors

Many people have heard that August is the best time of year for seeing meteors. The reason is the reliable Perseid meteor shower, which reaches a climax about August 12 or 13. For more about these meteors see page 74.

OPHIUCHUS

SCUTUM

SERPENS
(CAUDA)

the Teaspoon

Trifid Nebula

Lagoon Nebula

SAGITTARIUS

SCORPIUS

With the book 12 inches from your eye,
this is how large Sagittarois really looks.

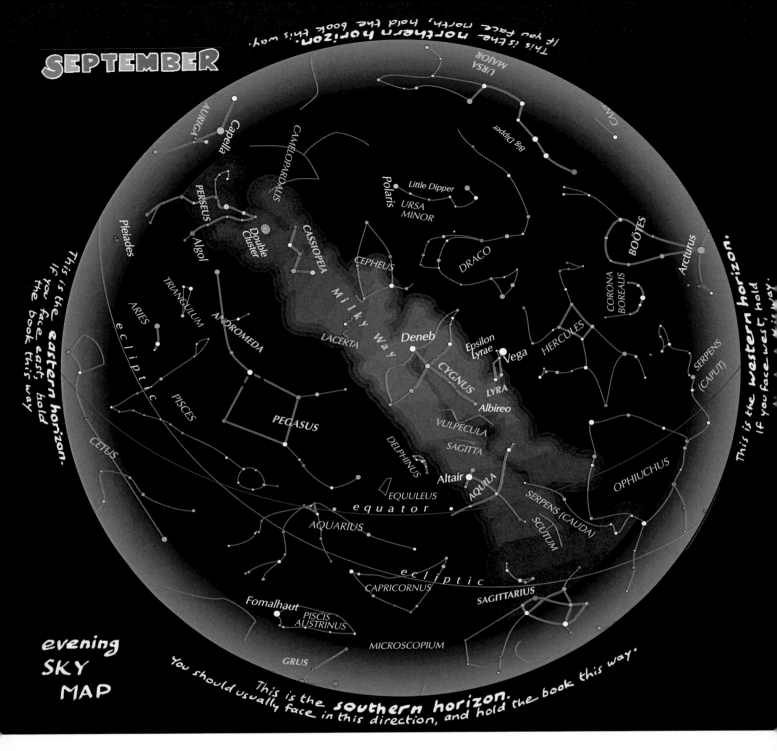

SEPTEMBER

URSA MAJOR

Capella
AURIGA

PERSEUS
Double Cluster
Pleiades
Algol
CASSIOPEIA
CAMELOPARDALIS

TRIANGULUM
ARIES
ANDROMEDA

Polaris
Little Dipper
URSA MINOR
CEPHEUS
DRACO
Big Dipper

BOÖTES
Arcturus
CORONA BOREALIS

ecliptic
PISCES
PEGASUS
LACERTA
Milky Way

Deneb
Epsilon Lyrae
Vega
CYGNUS
HERCULES
LYRA
Albireo
VULPECULA
SAGITTA
DELPHINUS

SERPENS (CAPUT)

CETUS
equator
EQUULEUS
Altair
AQUILA
OPHIUCHUS
SERPENS (CAUDA)
SCUTUM

AQUARIUS

ecliptic
CAPRICORNUS
SAGITTARIUS

Fomalhaut
PISCIS AUSTRINUS
MICROSCOPIUM
GRUS

evening
SKY
MAP

The autumn equinox

Since the spring equinox in March, the Sun has been moving along the northern half of the ecliptic, and shining more on Earth's northern hemisphere. After three months, at the summer solstice in June, the Sun was at its northernmost, traveling overhead for places like Mexico, southern Egypt, and southern China. After that, for the next three months, the Sun moved down the part of the ecliptic that slopes southward through Gemini, Cancer, and Leo. So it was slightly farther south in the sky each day, and the days got gradually shorter.

On September 23 (in some years September 22) the Sun comes to the second place where the ecliptic crosses the equator. This point is in Virgo, and is off our sky map to the right—of course, because the sky map shows the sky about three hours after sunset.

At the moment of crossing the equator, the Sun is overhead on the equator of the Earth, so it is shining equally on the northern and southern hemispheres. And the days and nights are the same length, 12 hours each. (*Equinox* means "equal night.") After this, for us in the northern hemisphere, the days keep getting shorter and cooler, as winter approaches.

The words *fall* and *autumn* mean the same. Nowadays Americans use *fall* and British people use *autumn*, but most of them understand the word used by the others.

The northern Milky Way

Upward from the line of Andromeda we come again to the line of the Milky Way. This is the other slope of the "bridge" that arches over from the summer Milky Way (below Cygnus) to the winter (Auriga-Taurus) part, which has now reappeared from the east.

The bridge here becomes narrow, and in some places it almost breaks. But it is easy to follow with your eye because it is strewn with fairly bright stars. These form Cassiopeia and Perseus. And, like the Sagittarius and Cygnus parts, it is full of clumps and clusters of stars that you can explore with binoculars or telescope.

When we look toward the Andromeda Galaxy, we are seeing it at a low angle from our own galaxy.

Rather like peering under a table and seeing the seat of a chair on the far side.

Cassiopeia

Cassiopeia is one of the groups of stars known to many people. Perhaps it comes fourth in popularity after the Big Dipper, Orion, and the Pleiades.

The reason is its easily recognizable shape: like a W. People argue about whether it is a W or an M! Of course it depends on which way you are facing, and which position it's in as it revolves around the Pole.

To the Greeks it was neither a W nor an M but a chair. You can see the lines as the chair's back, seat, front legs, and footstool. In the story we told last month, Queen Cassiopeia was one of the bad characters. As punishment she was tied to her throne, which was then set close to the Pole of the sky. So it whirls around the Pole, and Cassiopeia has to spend half of every day upside down.

Cassiopeia and Ursa Major are the two brightest of the "circumpolar" constellations, and they whirl around opposite to each other. At times when Ursa Major is on the low side (as it is in the evening sky from about August to December), trees or haze may prevent you from using its two Pointer stars to find the Pole Star. So you can use Cassiopeia instead. The trouble is that none of its stars line up to point at the pole. The best I can suggest is that if the "W" of stars forms the arms of a tennis player serving, then the Pole Star is the ball he has tossed up with his left hand.

The Navajo Indians call Ursa Major "The Whirling Male" and Cassiopeia "The Whirling Female." Coincidence?—or could the constellation of the Whirling Queen date back to a time before the ancestors of Indians and Europeans went their separate ways?

Perseus

Perseus is the next part of the Milky Way along from Cassiopeia, down and left (we should really say south-east).

In the short stretch of Milky Way between Cassiopeia and Perseus is a famous object that you can see in a telescope, and even dimly with naked eyes on a fine night. It is the Double Cluster: two large clusters of stars, close to each other and very far away from us.

Another way to find Perseus is that the leg of his girl-friend Andromeda points to him. The more ways you have to connect constellations together, the surer you will be of finding them.

Perseus continued ➞

The stars of Perseus really look like just a forked twig. You have to imagine the picture of the hero. There is a short line of stars in the Milky Way, making his helmeted head. Then there is the brightest star, called Mirfak. From Mirfak there are two branches leading south out of the Milky Way. The longer one is Perseus's body. The shorter is his left arm, and ends at the second brightest star in the constellation, called Algol.

The demon star

Algol represents the head of the Gorgon Medusa, which Perseus is carrying in his hand. You remember that, in the Greek story, poor Medusa was so fearfully ugly that the sight of her paralysed people. The name Algol which the Arabs later gave to the star means "the ghoul": a ghost that ate dead bodies. So, one way and another, this star has always been thought of as evil—the "Demon Star."

In 1782, 18-year-old John Goodricke studied and explained Algol. Every 2 days, 20 hours, and 49 minutes—exactly—it dims for about 10 hours. It is an "eclipsing binary": two stars very close together. As they revolve around each other, the larger and dimmer star blocks the other's light.

We may guess that in several parts of the ancient world people noticed Algol "winking," and that was why it got the reputation of being wicked.

Back to where we started

The curve of the main branch of Perseus leads down to the Pleiades. They could be in the constellation Perseus, and represent his foot. But, as we saw in January, they are regarded as being in the hump of the bull-constellation, Taurus.

We are back to the stars we discovered at the beginning of the year.

Cetus the whale

Two more "watery" constellations bring us even nearer to our January start.

Cetus means "whale" in Latin. The creature that attacked Andromeda in the story could have been a whale or a mythical sea-monster. It isn't easy to make the sky-creature into a whale: he has a fan-shaped head and a bell-shaped lower end. The "clapper" of the bell, or tail of the animal, is the constellation's brightest star, Diphda.

The "wonder" star

In Cetus's throat is a star called Mira, "the wonderful" (in Latin). You can see it only for a few weeks each year; the rest of the time it is too dim. When it was discovered in 1596, no other variable stars were known, so it made a great impression.

It doesn't vary for the same reason as Algol. It varies because it is a "red giant" that keeps brightening tremendously and fading back. Many other "Mira-type" variable stars have since been discovered.

The River Eridanus

Greek legends told of a river called Eridanus somewhere in Europe, but no one was sure where it was. The sky river is a long winding line of mostly faint stars. Cetus seems to be splashing into one bend of the river.

The river flows downward to end below the horizon at a very bright star, too far south to see from North America or Europe. Its name is Achernar, "end of the river" in Arabic.

As for the river's source, it is a star just up and right from Rigel. It is called Cursa, because some storytellers say it is not a spring of water, but a "stool" on which Orion can place his foot.

The Geminids and Ursids

These two meteor showers happen about December 13 and 22. (As with other showers, the dates when they are at their best can be a day earlier or later, because of our calendar with its leap-days in some years.) I once stayed out all night watching the well-known Geminids. It would be even more heroic to do that with the Ursids, because they come at midwinter, on or about the longest night.

For more about the meteor showers, see page 74.

The winter solstice

Midwinter is December 21 or 22. That is, the northern part of the Earth is tilted most away from the Sun. The Sun appears at the most southerly part of the ecliptic, in Sagittarius. It sets soonest and rises latest; we have the shortest days and longest nights.

If you were to stay outside for all of this longest time of darkness—about 14 hours—you would see almost all of the sky that you now know: just about everything except Sagittarius (where the Sun now is) and Scorpius its close neighbor. And a part of the sky will come around twice. In the early evening the strong man, Hercules, goes down in the west; and before dawn you would see him climb into view again over the eastern horizon. —Note: I do **not** advise staying out all of this midwinter night!

The Sun on the southernmost part of the ecliptic in December

CASSIOPEIA

CAMELOPARDALIS

With the book 12 inches from your eye,
this is how large Perseus really looks.

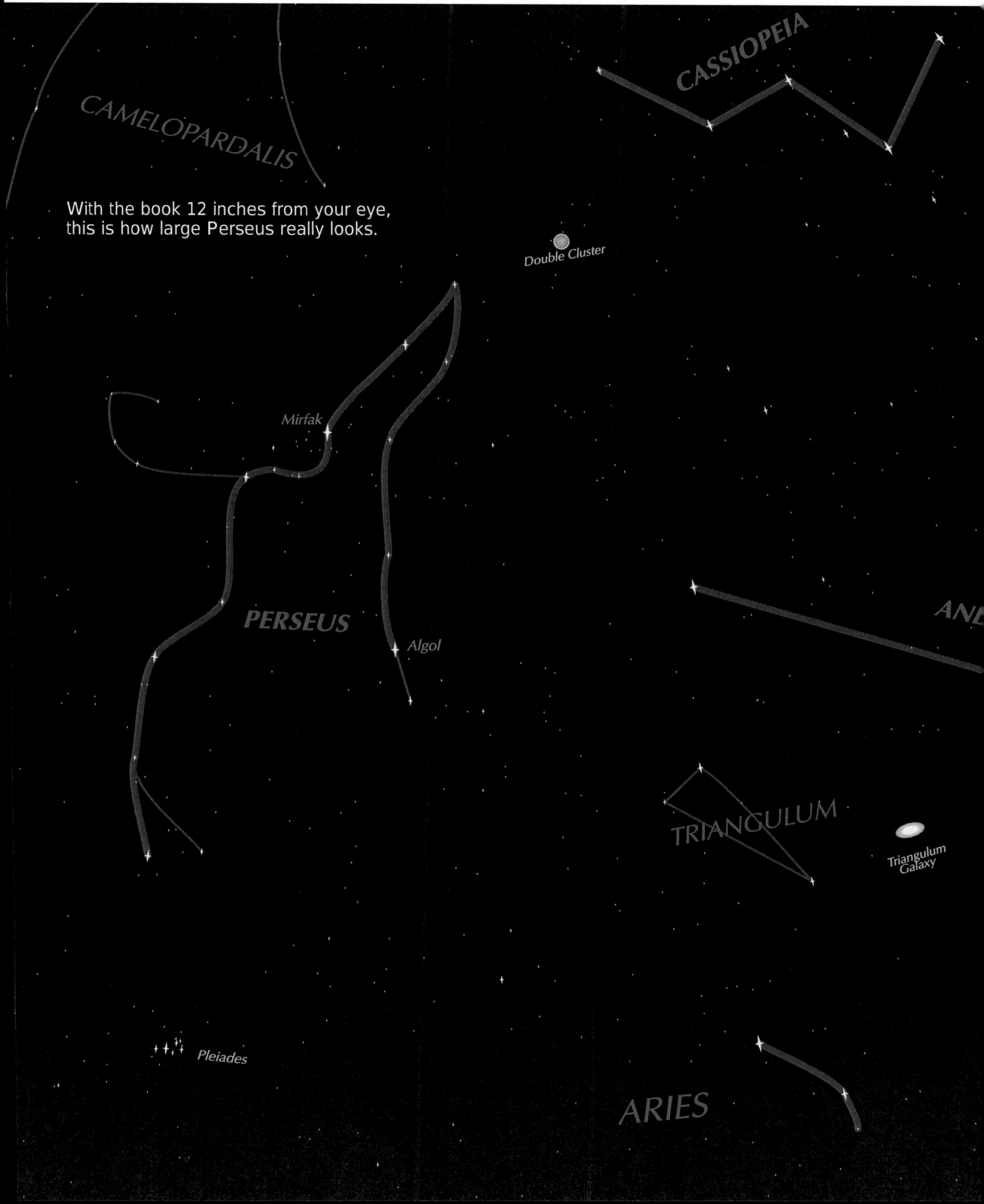

Double Cluster

Mirfak

PERSEUS

Algol

AN

TRIANGULUM

Triangulum
Galaxy

Pleiades

ARIES

MORE EXPLANATIONS

You are in space

If Earth, Sun, and Moon vanished, you would find yourself floating in black space. You would see stars all around you.

The stars are huge fiery

globes, but so far away that they look like mere points.

This picture is simple: just you, space, and the stars! It is Earth, Sun and Moon that make it more complicated.

Earth and Sun

You are not floating alone in space. You are on a solid globe, the Earth.

And the Earth is near one of the stars: the Sun. Because this star is much nearer than all the others, it looks much larger and brighter.

A thing to remember about diagrams like this is that the *scale* is wrong. That means that the sizes and distances do not have the right proportions.

For instance you are perhaps between 5 and 6 feet tall, which is about a thousandth of a mile, so if the picture were to scale you would be far too small to see. Here are the real sizes and distances:

your height in miles   about ⅟₁₀₀₀
width of Earth   8,000
distance Earth to Sun 93,000,000
width of Sun   800,000

In the drawing, the Earth is about 2 millimeters or 8/100 of an inch wide. On that scale the Sun ought to be 8 inches wide; and it ought to be 26 yards away! And you ought to be a hundred-millionth of an inch high! That's why we can't do the drawing with true scale.

Earth is moving

Our Earth is moving in two ways. It is traveling around the Sun in a circle; and it is also spinning.

The proper words for these two motions are *revolving* and *rotating*.

Notice that the Earth revolves and rotates in the same direction. If you look from above (that is, from the side we call the north), they are both "counter-clockwise," or in the opposite direction to a clock.

clock

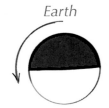

Earth

The solid Earth and the horizon

Though the Earth is so small compared with other things in space, it is very large compared with us human beings. We are so small that to us, standing on the Earth, it doesn't seem to curve at all. It just seems like a huge flat floor disappearing into the distance.

In this picture you are still

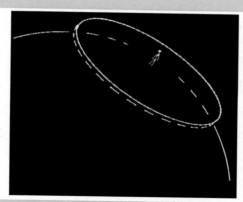

drawn much too large. The Earth's surface is curved, but to you it looks like a flat plane. It seems to end at the line called the "horizon."

So the Earth blocks out half of space for you. It is the reason why you forget you are floating in space. Your surroundings seem to be divided into two halves: below you the solid Earth; above you, the half called the "sky."

The blue sky

Well, you still should be able to see half of the universe, looking like a black space, with the stars in it, and one very near and bright star—the Sun. But no: the sky is bright blue. You can see the Sun in it, but no other stars. Why is this?

The Earth happens to be wrapped in an atmosphere of air. As the Sun's light comes through this, most of it travels straight, but some of it, especially the blue part of the light, bounces in all directions off the particles of air. So, besides the light coming straight from the Sun, you see a

lot of other light (mostly blue) coming at you from all over the sky.

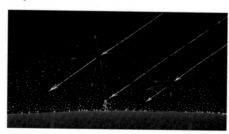

This explains, too, why the light coming straight from the Sun looks slightly yellow instead of white: some of the blue has been taken out of it.

The light of each star is also

coming to you, but is lost in the scattered sunlight. It is impossible to tell which point of light is the star's.

(Not quite impossible. By knowing exactly where to look, people have been able to see the brightest stars through telescopes even in the blue sunlit sky.)

So the Earth, the Earth's atmosphere, and the Sun are preventing you from looking out into space and seeing the stars. But don't get too annoyed with the Earth, the Earth's atmosphere, and the Sun—without them you wouldn't be alive!

Day and night

As the Earth rotates (spins), it carries you around out of sight of the Sun. The time when the Sun is in the half of the sky that you can see is day. The time when it is not is night. Duh!

In the night, you are still looking through the air, but it is not filled with scattered sunlight. So

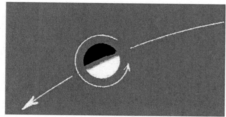

you can see the stars. The day is the time for getting on with activities on the Earth; the night

is the time for looking out into space. (And for some sleeping, if you like!)

In a way, instead of thinking of night as a time, you can think of it as a place: the side of the Earth facing away from the Sun. After all, when it's night for you it's day for people on the other side of the Earth.

The views at evening, midnight, and morning

Look at the diagram and think about it.

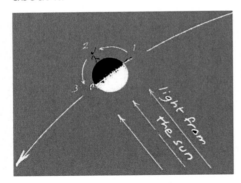

Person 1 (whose name is Eve) is standing on the part of the Earth that is just moving out of sunlight into darkness. In other words, it is sunset for her. (It is around 6 p.m., 6 o'clock in the evening.) Remember that we have had to draw her much, much larger than she really is. She should be just an invisible speck! If she looks along the plane of her horizon, she sees the Sun disappearing.

She is on the backward side of the Earth as it travels along. If she looks straight out into space—that is, straight upward—then she is looking *back* along the direction the Earth has been traveling.

Person 3 (whose name happens to be Dawn) is standing on the opposite side of the Earth. She is, at this moment, being carried around into view of the Sun. In other words, she is seeing the Sun rise. Where she is, it is about 6 a.m. (6 o'clock in the morning). She is on the front of the Earth—like standing on the bow of a ship. If she looks upward, she is looking *forward* along the Earth's orbit.

Person 2 (whose name is Minnie) is on the part of the Earth that is facing straight away from the Sun. For her it is mid-night, 12 p.m. She is on the outer side of the Earth as it travels along. She has the best view of the stars.

Of course, these three people might be one person at different times. At 6 p.m. you are standing where person 1 is, watching the Sun set. Six hours later (at midnight), the spinning of the Earth has brought you around to where person 2 is. For another six hours you keep standing there (or sitting) and the Earth keeps turning, and there you are at the position of person 3: it is sunrise.

So the Earth, with you on it, is all the time turning from right to left. You keep seeing stars farther to the left. If you forget that this is what is really happening, then it looks to you as if the stars are slowly moving around past you the opposite way, from left to right.

About 9 in the evening

Most of us humans have the strange habit of going to bed well after sunset, and getting up at or after sunrise. This means we are awake in the early part of the night, but not the later part. So the usual time we look at the stars is between sunset and the time we go to bed.

Imagine another person in the last picture, half way between persons 1 and 2. Her name is Nona. She is standing at the place on Earth where it is about 9 p.m.—half way between sun-set and midnight. She is a typi-cal stargazer looking at the evening sky. If she looks upward, she is looking not straight back along the Earth's orbit, nor straight outward into space away from the Sun, but at an angle in between.

In our sky maps for each month, we show Nona's view of the sky for that month. It is the half of the universe that you can see about 9 p.m. in the evenings about the middle of that month.

The night sky changes through the year

The Earth takes a year to go around the Sun. In fact that is what "year" means: the time the Earth takes to go around the Sun.

Here is a larger picture showing the Earth at its positions in the middle of January, February, and so on—12 places in its orbit around the Sun.

Each time, Nona is standing stargazing at 9 o'clock in the evening. From month to month, her view into space swings farther to the left. By the end of the year, her view has swung all the way around.

So the same kind of change happens through the night and through the year. Through the night, the Earth keeps turning to the left (counter-clockwise), so

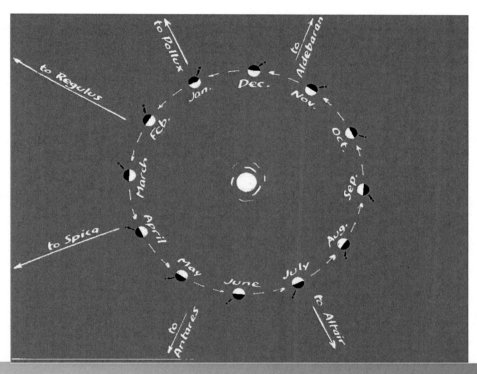

our view swings to the left, and new stars keep coming into view on the left. And through the year, the Earth keeps circling around the Sun to the left, so that the view at a certain time—such as Nona's view at 9 p.m.—keeps swinging to the left, and new stars keep appearing at the left.

The arrows around the edge point to a few of the stars. (Remember, they are very far away.) In January, Nona can see the star Aldebaran high in the middle of the sky at 9 p.m. (Look at the January sky map: there it is.) She cannot see Altair, because it is in the same direction as the Sun: in other words, it is in the sky only in daytime. Also she cannot see Antares, because at 9 p.m. the Earth is hiding it from her. (If she pointed to it, she would be pointing down into the ground under her feet.) But if she stays up watching all night, she will see it come into view. If she keeps watching only at 9 p.m., then in July she will see Antares in the middle of her view, and in August and September she will see Altair there. (Again look at the sky maps.)

On the round Earth

We have shown the figures of Nona and the others as if they are standing on the middle part of the Earth—the equator. But people live all over the round Earth, not just on the equator.

Here is a picture of the way it is for a Polar Bear who lives at the north pole; a Tiger who lives at the equator; and a Penguin who lives at the south pole. Also

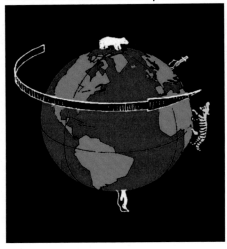

a European, about half way between the equator and the north pole. He is typical of many of us who live in Europe, North America, or other parts of the northern hemisphere.

Each of them is of course tremendously smaller than we have had to draw them. Each feels that he is on a large flat surface, and each feels that "down" is the direction toward the middle of the Earth.

For each of them, the Earth is spinning in the same way, and

the stars are staying out in their places in the distance. But for each of them it **looks** as if the stars are moving differently.

For the Polar Bear, it looks as if the stars are going around in horizontal circles, staying at the same heights above the horizon. And he can see only the stars in the northern half of space; he can never see any of the southern ones.

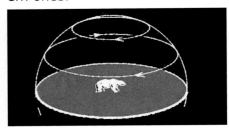

The view of the Penguin is exactly the opposite. He sees only the stars in the southern half of space. He sees them going around in circles above him, but in the opposite direction. (Things don't look to him upside-down. "Down" is for him, as for anyone else, the direction toward the middle of the Earth.)

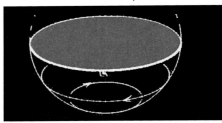

The Tiger can see all the stars, though only half at one time. They seem to come up on

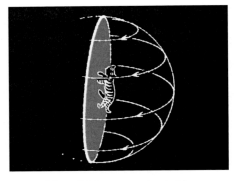

one side of him, go straight over his head, and go down on the other side.

The Polar Bear, Tiger, and Penguin are in special places, where the view of the stars is simple. For everybody else, somewhere between the equator and one of the poles, it is not so simple. It is something between the way it appears at the equator and at the pole.

The view of the European is what we showed at the beginning of the book. The stars appear to move not in horizontal circles as they do for the Polar Bear, nor in vertical circles passing overhead as for the Tiger, but in a way between these two: in **sloping** circles.

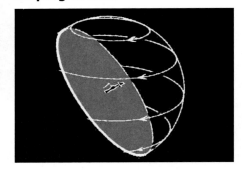

The tilted Earth

As the Earth flies in its orbit around the Sun, it does not stand up straight. It leans over, at an angle of 23½ degrees. It doesn't lean like this—

—but the same way all the time.

This is what makes the times of the year different for us. It is what causes the **seasons**.

The seasons

December is our name for the time when the northern hemisphere of the Earth is tilted most away from the Sun. June is the opposite time, when the northern hemisphere is tilted toward the Sun. March and September are the times half way between, when the northern hemisphere is not tilted away or toward the Sun.

In June, the Sun is shining most directly onto the north-ern hemisphere. So this is the middle of what we call summer. And December is the middle of winter, for the northern hemisphere.

Remember that for the southern hemisphere it is the other way around. In countries like Argentina and New Zealand, December is the middle of summer, because the southern hemisphere is tilted toward the Sun, and the Sun is shining most directly on it.

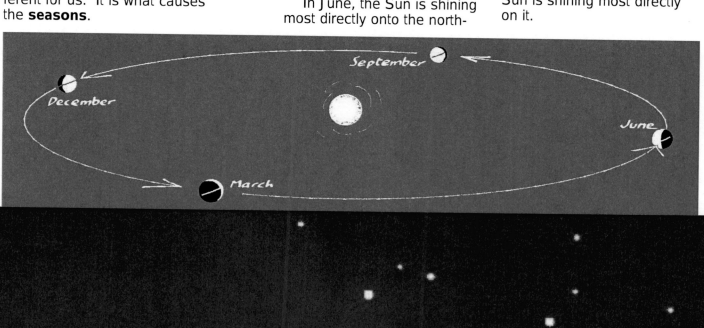

THE MOON

Around the Sun goes the Earth, and around the Earth goes the Moon. The Sun puts out light, but Earth and Moon are solid lumps that shine only because of the Sun's light hitting them.

Sizes and distances

Sun's width (miles)	about 800,000
Earth's width	8,000
Moon's width	2,000
Sun to Earth	93,000,000
Earth to Moon	240,000

So the Moon is about 4 times smaller than the Earth in width, and about 400 times smaller than the Sun.

But it is also about 400 times nearer! So the Moon and Sun look to us the same size, almost exactly.

The long diagram down the side of the page is to scale: Earth and Moon have the right sizes in relation to each other and are the right distance apart.

The Moon's journey

So much for distances; what about times? The Earth goes around the Sun in a year, that is, about 365½ days. The Moon goes around the Earth in about 29½ days. So, each year, the Moon goes around us about 12½ times.

All these "abouts" are because the real numbers are not neat. It might be nice if we could say that the Moon is exactly 2,000 miles wide, or that the Earth goes around the Sun in 360 days and the Moon around the Earth in 30 days (exactly 12 times a year). But that would be like expecting every rock to be square or every person to have one million hairs. Nature is not like that.

Ancient people noticed the Moon going around the sky about 12 times a year, so they divided the year into 12 "moonths." But, as you now know, this wasn't accurate, and months are out of step with the real movements of the Moon. A real cycle of the Moon—a journeying of it around us once—is called a lunation (from *luna*, the Latin word for "Moon").

Here is a picture of one about-29½-day lunation. The scale is reduced: we show the Moon 4 times nearer to Earth than it really is. The bright sides of Earth and Moon are that way because light is hitting them from the Sun, far off to the right.

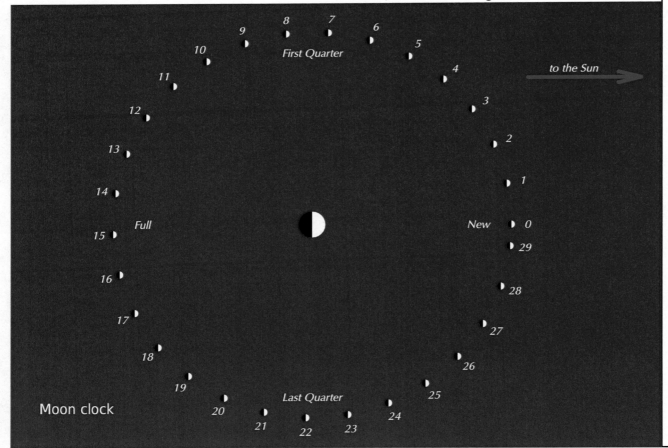

Moon clock

Earth

Moon

is a star. It's about 93,000,000 miles from us, and 865,000 miles wide. It contains about 740 times as much matter as the rest of the solar system put together.

It is about three quarters hydrogen, and a quarter helium, with a tiny bit of other elements such as oxygen, carbon and iron. (But this "tiny bit" amounts to nearly 6,000 times as much matter as there is in the Earth.) The Sun rotates in about 25 days, though as it isn't solid parts of it churn around at different speeds.

In the Sun's core (which is about 400,000 miles wide), tremendous pressure keeps up a non-stop nuclear reaction, fusing 600 million tons of hydrogen atoms into helium every second. The heat from this takes many thousand years to work its way up through the Sun, and comes out of the top layer as light. So this layer, which is what we can see, is called the *photosphere*, "light-sphere." Escaping from it, the light takes only 8 minutes to reach Earth.

If you boil water in a pan, you will see blobs of hot water bulge up at the top and drop back as they cool. This is called "convection," and it happens on the Sun. Large photographs show that the surface is broken into these blobs, called "granules." There are always about 4 million of them, Each lasts a few minutes and is about the size of Alaska!

Among the granules are **sunspots**, which can be up to 100,000 miles wide and are darker, because they are cooler. So they can be seen more easily and have been known about for many centuries. There is a "sunspot cycle" of about 11 years (though it varies). The sunspots almost die out, then they start appearing again. This has a lot of effects on the radiation coming from the Sun, and on life on Earth.

Above the Sun's surface is a thin layer called the chromosphere, "color-sphere," which you may glimpse as a little red flash just as an eclipse of the Sun becomes total. Above that is the corona, which makes the glorious display during total eclipse. But this corona that you see is only the inner part of the Sun's atmosphere. Out through it blows the "solar wind" of particles streaming from the Sun. The solar wind blows out past all the planets, all the way to about 100 times the Earth's distance. There it meets the space between the stars, thinly filled with other particles. The enormous bubble formed by the solar wind is called the heliosphere, "the Sun's domain."

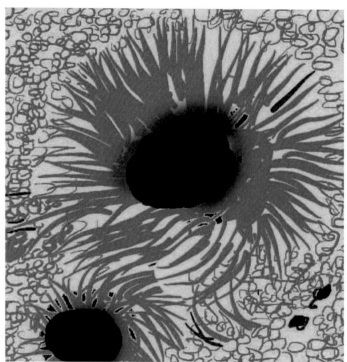

Granules, and some sunspots of various sizes. Many of the granules are as large as Alaska. Really the sunspots are dark only in comparison with the rest of the Sun.

Stars are suns . . .

But instead of talking in a general way, let's jump straight to what I found most fun when I was first getting to know the stars: which are the brightest?

The Top Twenty

1. Sirius. We got to know it in February; look again at that page.

2. Canopus. This great star is too far south to see from most of the U.S.A. or Europe. Look at the February sky map. If you could dig an enormous canyon in the southern horizon, just about directly south of Sirius, you would see Canopus through the bottom of it.

3. Alpha Centauri is even farther south, so until recent times it was unknown to the people of northern countries. That is why they have no real name for it. **Alpha** is the name of α, the first letter of the Greek alphabet, so what it means is that this is the brightest or "A" star in the constellation Centaurus. What's a centaur? A half-man-half-horse; see what we said in August about Sagittarius, who is also one of these mythical beings. A bit of Centaurus shows at the southern edge of our sky map for May, but Alpha Centauri is a long way south of that. It is bright because it is the **nearest star**: only 4.4 light-years away. Actually it's more complicated than that. This is a star-system: there are two stars close together, one of them about the same size, brightness, and color as our Sun, the other slightly smaller and more orange. And some distance from them is a third star, a "red dwarf." This tiny star (which you can't see in any ordinary telescope) is nearer to us than the other two—only 4.2 light-years—so it is **the nearest star of all**. It is known as Proxima Centauri. **Proxima** means "nearest" in Latin.

4. Arcturus, the golden star in

the middle of the June sky. Since Sirius, Canopus, and Alpha Centauri are all south of the sky's equator, Arcturus is the brightest star in the northern celestial hemisphere.

5. Vega (see "The Summer Triangle," in August) and,

6. Capella (see "Auriga, the Charioteer," in February). These two are almost as bright as Arcturus. It used to be thought that Vega was the brightest north-hemisphere star; according to modern measurements Arcturus is the winner by a hair. For people in the United States and Europe, Vega and Capella are the two great "overhead" stars: Vega in summer, and Capella in winter.

7. Rigel in Orion (see January). This and number 19 (Deneb) are different from the others in the list: they are super-powerful stars, very far away. If we could travel the 770 light-years to Rigel, we would see that it is about **30,000 times** brighter than our Sun.

8. Procyon, the "alpha" star of Canis Minor (see February).

9. Achernar, another far-south star, at the southern end of the river-constellation Eridanus (see December).

10. Betelgeuse, the first star you learned in January; the most famous of the kind called "red giants." It is more than 400 light-years away, and huge—probably about 600 times wider than the Sun! If it was where the Sun is, Earth would be deep inside it. But it is rather dim and cool for its size, and it slowly throbs like a heart, so that its brightness varies: sometimes it really ought to be higher on our list, sometimes lower. At any rate it is not as bright as Rigel. Yet because of its redness and being higher in the sky it catches the eye more; so it received the title Alpha Orionis, "star A of Orion," while Rigel has to be content with Beta.

11. Beta Centauri. As its name shows, this is the "B" star

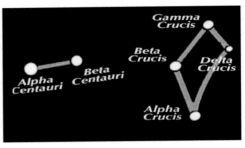

in the far-south constellation of the Centaur. It and Alpha Centauri make a striking pair, and if this book were mainly for people in the southern hemisphere of the Earth we would have much more to say about them.

12. Altair, the alpha star of Aquila the Eagle: see September.

13. Alpha Crucis, "Alpha of the Cross." In the deep-south skies next to Alpha and Beta Centauri there are four stars, really in a diamond shape rather than a cross, and two of them get into the top twenty (see number 20).

14. Aldebaran, Betelgeuse's orange neighbor in Taurus: see January.

15. Spica, the white star in Virgo: see June.

16. Antares, "rival of Mars," the red giant that is the heart of the Scorpion: see July.

17. Pollux, twin brother of Castor (see February). This is a case rather like Betelgeuse and Rigel: though Pollux is brighter, he gets the Greek letter Beta. Probably this is because when story-tellers tell the stories about the twins, they always call them "Castor and Pollux," not the other way around.

18. Fomalhaut, a lonely bright star, quite far south but not too far for us to see from mid-northern countries: see the "Southern Fish" in October.

19. Deneb, or Alpha Cygni: see the "Summer Triangle" in August. Though near the bottom of this list, it is really by far the greatest star in it, farther and brighter even than Rigel.

20. Beta Crucis, the fourth in

the brilliant group of stars so far south that northern people don't have real names for them: see Alpha Crucis and Alpha and Beta Centauri.

21, a bonus. **Regulus**, heart of Leo the lion (see April). Somehow we always think of it as being in the first rank of stars; its name means "king" or "ruler"; it dominates its part of the sky; so we could hardly offend its dignity by leaving it out.

22, another bonus: **Adhara**. Few people know this star separately; it is merely the brightest of the three at the lower end of Canis Major (it is the one on the right, making the dog's leg). We put it in because otherwise we can't include:

23. **Castor**, the twin of Pollux. And maybe we should have included **the Sun** as number 1.

Magnitude

Even though we squeezed Regulus and Castor in, a lot of the stars you know are not in the Top Twenty list. Perhaps you were surprised that the Pole Star is not there, or any of the stars in the Big Dipper or the Square of Pegasus. They would have to be in our list of the hundred or so next brightest stars.

The ancient Greek astronomers made lists, dividing the stars into six groups according to brightness. The first group was about the same as our Top Twenty. These were called the stars "of the first magnitude." *Magnitude* means literally "bigness," and it seemed likely that the brightest stars were the largest.

The second group consisted of stars not quite so bright, such as the Pole Star, and the other main stars in Orion. These were stars "of the second magnitude." And so on down to the stars of the sixth magnitude: these were the dimmest that can be seen with the naked eye.

We still use this system, saying that Deneb is a "first-magnitude star," and the Pole Star's brightness is "second magnitude." But we can now measure the brightness of the stars more exactly. So, instead of the six rough groups, we have numbers: Deneb's magnitude is actually 1.25. The Pole Star's is 1.97, so it is nearer to 2 than 1.

With telescopes we can see stars much fainter than the 6th-magnitude ones that are just visible to the eye. So their magnitudes might be 9.1, 14.5, and so on.

Things to remember about the way *magnitude* is used in astronomy:

—It describes brightness, not size. Brighter stars are *not* necessarily larger. They may be more powerful, or just nearer.

—The *smaller* the number, the brighter the star. A star of magnitude 1 is brighter than a star of magnitude 2.

As for what magnitude means in terms of real brightness: a star of magnitude 1 is about 2½ times brighter than a star of magnitude 2. So it is about 2½ times 2½ brighter than one of magnitude 3; that is, about 6¼ times. Not a very handy system, but we're stuck with it.

Real brightness

Here are our Top Twenty stars arranged in order of how bright they really are. We also tell how far away they are.

1. **Deneb.** Perhaps 170,000 times as bright as the Sun; perhaps 3,000 light-years away.
2. **Rigel.** 28,000 times; 770 light-years away.
3. **Canopus.** 9,000 times; 313 light-years.
4. **Beta Centauri.** 8,000 times; 525 light-years.
5. **Antares.** 8,000 times; 600 light-years.
6. **Betelgeuse.** 6,000 times; 430 light-years.
7. **Alpha Crucis.** 3,000 times; 320 light-years.
8. **Adhara.** 2,500 times; 430 light-years.
9. **Beta Crucis.** 2,000 times; 350 light-years.
10. **Spica.** 1,500 times; 260 light-years.
11. **Achernar.** 750 times; 140 light-years.
12. **Aldebaran.** 100 times; 65 light-years.
13. **Regulus.** 90 times; 77 light-years.
14. **Capella.** 90 times; 42 light-years.
15. **Arcturus.** 80 times; 36 light-years.
16. **Vega.** 30 times; 25 light-years.
17. **Castor.** 30 times; 52 light-years.
18. **Pollux.** 20 times; 34 light-years.
19. **Sirius.** 14 times; 8.6 light-years.
20. **Fomalhaut.** 12 times; 25 light-years.
21. **Altair.** 8 times; 17 light-years.
22. **Procyon.** 5 times; 11 light-years.
23. **Alpha Centauri.** 1½ times; 4.4 light-years.
24. **The Sun.** 8 *light-minutes.*

You have to remember that these are only the stars in our Top Twenty list. There are millions of other stars that could be added between them. For instance the Pole Star is 1,600 times as bright as the Sun, and 430 light-years away; this combination of brightness and distance makes it only about the 46th brightest star in our sky. Very far off there are rare stars that seem very dim but actually are brighter even than Deneb.

Star colors

The stars do have colors, though pale ones. They are most noticeable if the stars are bright, like reddish Betelgeuse and bluish Rigel in Orion; or if stars of

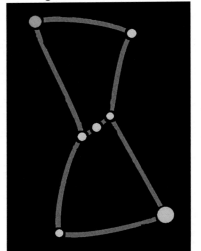

different color are close together, like the yellow and blue "double star" Albireo in Cygnus.

The reason for a

star's color is the temperature of its surface.

If you heat something such as an iron poker, it begins to glow red. That's why we use the phrase "red hot," and think of red as being a warm color. But if you go on heating the poker, it turns orange and then yellow. So, really, red is the *least* hot color! It is the color things turn when you *begin* to heat them.

The stars are all hot. The least hot ones are red, the next hotter ones orange, and so on.

You probably know the colors of the spectrum, which are mixed together to make white light and appear separately in the rainbow:

red, orange, yellow, green, blue, violet. As stars get hotter they move along this spectrum, from red toward blue.

So why aren't there any **green stars??**

A star isn't putting out light of just one color, It's putting out a lot of one color and less of the neighboring colors. The stars of middle temperature, such as our Sun, are putting out most of their light in the middle of the spectrum: yellow and green. But they also put out some of the other colors; so the mixture looks white.

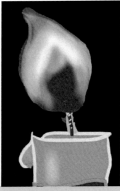

The coolest part of a flame, at the edge, is red.

Dwarfs and giants

On a beach, you might see billions of grains of sand, hundreds of shells, and a few rocks. This is the way it is with stars. There are many more little than big ones.

Probably most of the stars in the universe are *red dwarfs*: stars much smaller than the Sun, burning slowly. Then there is a

middle number of middle-sized stars, such as the Sun, Alpha Centauri, and Sirius. The rarest stars are the very large ones: *blue giants* like Rigel and Deneb, and *red giants* like Betelgeuse and Antares.

But this is not the way it looks in the sky! Almost all the stars you can see with your naked eyes are larger than the Sun.

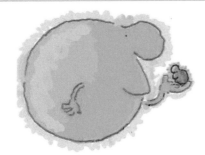

Most are giants. None are red dwarfs!

The red dwarfs are so small and dim that it takes the world's largest telescopes to find even the ones that are our nearest neighbors in space. The few giants shine so powerfully that we see them more easily than thousands of nearer stars.

Instead of the beach you could think of another picture. You are standing in a field. You see trees far away, but you don't see insects that are hovering a few yards from you

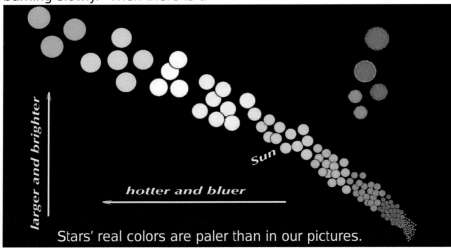

Stars' real colors are paler than in our pictures.

The nearest stars

Another list:

1. **Proxima Centauri**, the little red dwarf, which is 4.2 light-years away and is probably in a long slow orbit around Alpha Centauri.

2 and 3. **Alpha Centauri**, 4.4 light-years away. A double star; that's why I rank it as 2 and 3.

4. **Barnard's Star**, in the constellation Ophiuchus, another red dwarf, 6 light-years away.

5. A star called **Wolf 359,** meaning that it was number 359 in a list of stars discovered by an astronomer named Wolf. A red dwarf; in the Leo direction; 7.8 light-years away.

6. **Lalande 21185**, number 21185 in a list made by Lalande. In Leo; a red dwarf; 8.3 light-years away.

7 and 8. **Sirius** and the **companion of Sirius**. We haven't mentioned before that Sirius is a double star: close to the very bright star is a very faint one of the kind called a **white dwarf**. They are 8.6 light-years away.

9 and 10. **Luyten 726-8**, another double star, both red dwarfs; in Cetus, 8.7 light-years away.

11. **Ross 154**, red dwarf; in Sagittarius; 9.7 light-years.

12. **Ross 248**, red dwarf; in Andromeda; 10.3 light-years.

13. **Epsilon Eridani**, an orange star smaller than the Sun. It is star ε (the Greek letter epsilon) in Eridanus, and is 10.5 light-years away.

14. **Lacaille 9352**, a red dwarf, quite near to the direction of bright Fomalhaut; 10.7 light-years away.

15. **Ross 128**, red dwarf; in Virgo; 10.9 light-years.

16, 17, 18. Luyten 789-6; a group of at least three red dwarfs; in Aquarius; 11.3 light-years away.

19, 20. **Procyon** and its **companion**, another white dwarf like the companion of Sirius; 11.4 light-years away.

21, 22. **61 Cygni**, a pair of small orange stars in Cygnus; 11.4 light-years away.

Again, we should really put the Sun at the top of the list. It's certainly our nearest star, being only 8 light-**minutes** away.

The stars whose names are **underlined** are the only ones you could see with the naked eye. Of the rest, most are so faint that they can only be found among the millions of others on observatory photographs. Most of their "names" are just numbers in catalogs. We could go on and give a longer list, but still most of the stars would be little unheard-of ones.

Now you can see what we meant about dwarfs being the commonest stars, and giants the rarest. Most of these nearest stars are red dwarfs. The brightest nearby stars are middle-sized (Sun, Alpha Centauri, Sirius, Procyon). There are *no* giant stars near enough to be in our list! (In fact there are none nearer than about 35 light-years.)

The list of nearby stars gives a truer picture of what stars are like than the list of bright stars does. Other parts of our galaxy, far from us, probably contain about the same mixture, with a lot of red dwarfs, but out there we can see only the few giants.

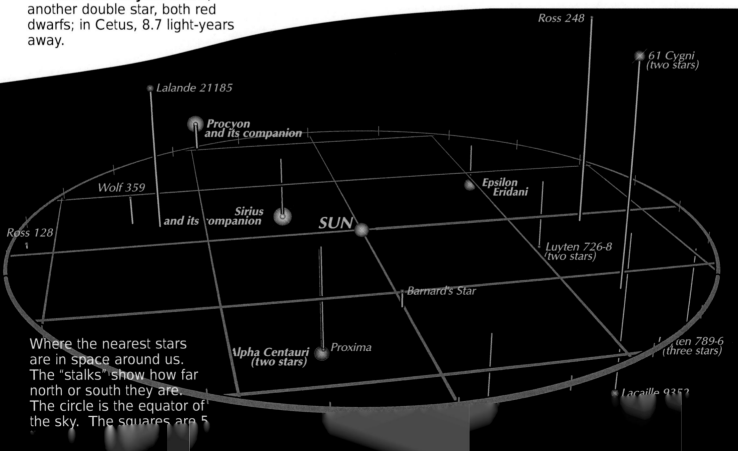

Where the nearest stars are in space around us. The "stalks" show how far north or south they are. The circle is the equator of the sky. The squares are 5

This is what scientists think happened.

The story of a star

There was a huge, very thin cloud of gas and dust. It gradually collapsed until the center of it became a very hot ball: the Sun. This was about 4,600,000,000 (4.6 billion) years ago.

Other parts of the cloud became the planets, asteroids, and comets.

The Sun burns (that is, turns hydrogen into helium) at a steady rate, and will go on about as long as it already has—another 5 billion years or so.

Then, when it has used up its hydrogen, it will go through faster processes and will swell up, perhaps out as far as the orbit of the Earth! Because of being so large, it will be much brighter, but also its surface will be cooler, therefore redder in color. The Sun will have become the kind of star called "red giant."

After that, it will go through other changes, including throwing out a lot of itself that becomes a cloud around it, called a "planetary nebula."

What is left of the Sun will shrink very tight, becoming a "white dwarf" (like the little companion stars to Sirius and Procyon). A white dwarf is extremely dense and hot, and will last almost forever before it finally stops shining.

Other stars were born in the same sort of way, some long before the Sun, some after. Some stars are in pairs close together, or groups of two or even more. Many are born in clusters (small clusters like the Pleiades and the Beehive, or huge globular clusters like the one in Hercules).

Some formed out of larger clouds and have more mass than the Sun. They burn faster, and are brighter and hotter, so that they are bluer in color. These are the "blue giants." They live a much shorter time—only a few million years!—then blow apart in a tremendous explosion, called a "supernova." What is left of a star after this shrinks to become something even smaller and denser than a white dwarf, called a "neutron star," or even to the incredibly dense thing called a "black hole."

Stars that are much smaller than the Sun don't get so hot, so they live a much longer time. These are the "red dwarfs" that are the commonest kind of star.

Exoplanets and exolife

For ages people wondered whether other stars have planets. Even the nearest stars are so far away that a planet is extremely difficult to see, being in just about the same place as the star and far dimmer.

But, starting in 1992, planets have been discovered in other ways, by clever measurements of the stars' movements, and by slight dimmings of stars as planets pass in front of them. And a few planets have actually been photographed as separate dots. We now know of more than a thousand "exoplanets."

Remember the layout of our own planetary system?—four small hard planets fairly close to the Sun, four soft giants farther out, and all in fairly circular orbits. We used to think there were good reasons for that, so that other systems would be similar. But they are of all sorts!

There are planets as large as Jupiter or much larger, and—unlike Jupiter—very close to their stars. There are planets in elliptical orbits, and stars with up

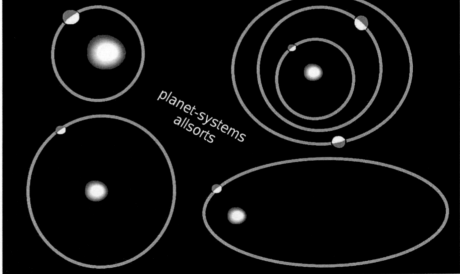

planet-systems allsorts

to seven planets and probably more to be found.

Is there life on any of them? Wouldn't we like to know! And we may be getting close.

It's still just possible that our Earth is unique. There are several lucky things about it that allowed life to get started. But there may be at least 100,000,000 planets in our Milky Way galaxy alone. How likely is it that no others got lucky?

It won't be easy to talk with alien beings. If they live at the very nearest star, it will take 4.2 years for a signal to reach them and the same for them to answer.

Our "city of stars"

The Sun is one of at least 200,000,000,000 stars (200 billion) in the Milky Way galaxy (which you got to know in February).

From our viewpoint inside it our galaxy looks like a band of soft light, with the nearer stars spread all around us.

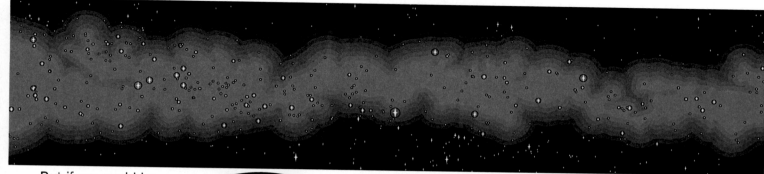

But if we could be outside it, our galaxy would look something like this:

It is about 100,000 light-years wide. It has spiral arms where there are more bright stars, clusters, and nebulas. Our Sun is in one of the arms, about 25,000 light-years from the galaxy's center (about where the cross is, though of course the Sun is far too small to see).

And galaxies beyond

There are two much smaller galaxies near ours, called the Large and Small Magellanic Clouds. This is because they were seen from Ferdinand Magellan's ship in 1520 when it was making the first voyage all around the world. They are far south in our sky—far below the bottom of our January sky map—so that to see them you'd have to go to South America.

Farther off, at about 2,500,000 light-years, is a spiral galaxy like ours, or even larger: the Great Galaxy in Andromeda, which we looked at in November. In large photographs it is amazingly beautiful and gives us an idea of what our own spiral galaxy is like.

Our Milky Way and these other galaxies and a few more form what is called the Local Group. It is on the edge of a larger swarm of galaxies, which can be seen in the constellations Virgo and Coma Berenices.

And there are more and more galaxies, out to vaster and vaster distances.

We live inside an explosion

The stars and the galaxies look to us as if they are standing still. But this is only because they are so far away. Really they are moving about at great speeds.

And it was discovered in the 1920s that the galaxies are all **moving away from us and from each other**. In other words, the universe is expanding!

What this must mean is that a long time ago everything was close together. It all started from an explosion, which is called the Big Bang. This is thought to have been 13,800,000,000 (13.8 billion) years ago.

The picture isn't really a bubble like this. There is no center; and there's no outside. Hard to understand.

Inconceivable

The distances and times we've talked about are **scary**. Nobody can really imagine them.

But think of this. Humans have been around for about 5,000,000 years. Till about 500 years ago, everybody believed that the Earth was the center of the universe, it didn't move, and the planets, Sun, and stars revolved around it and were not all that far away. The present picture is what humans have learned in less than 500 years. And science is going on so fast that we keep learning more. Our picture of the universe isn't likely to stay what it is now!

Good and bad skies.

Imagine you are in a place that is *open*: there are no nearby mountains, trees or buildings blocking your view. The sky is *dark*: there is no light in it except the stars' light. It is *clear*: there are no clouds, haze, or dirt. Now, that is a good sky!

Our ancestors often had that kind of sky. That is why they usually grew up knowing the stars better than we do.

Here are things that make the sky difficult for star-gazing, and what you can do about them:

—**Clouds.** Wait for better weather!

— **Obstructions,** such as trees and houses. Go somewhere else. But it may not be too bad if you can see quite a large part of the sky. You will have to work a bit harder, watching the stars as they move into that "window."

—**The Moon.** It goes through its four "phases" about a week apart: New Moon, First Quarter, Full Moon, Last Quarter. From around First Quarter till around Full Moon, the Moon is bright and high in the sky for most of the time between sunset and midnight. Its light is nothing like as bright as the Sun's, but it is enough to wipe out the dimmer stars. You can still look at the bright ones. Otherwise, look at a calendar for the date of Full Moon, and plan to do most of your star-gazing at *other* times.

—And:

Light pollution.

You'll have heard of many other kinds of pollution spoiling the modern world . . . but light pollution?

This is what star-lovers call the excessive light put out nowadays by such things as street lamps, all-night blinking signs, and lights on poles outside houses. Much of it is sheer waste. For instance lamps illuminating a parking lot do it better and more cheaply if they send all the light downward; but many of them send much of the light outward into your eyes and up into the sky.

The result of all this is that not only inside cities, but for fifty or more miles around many of them, the sky looks like mud, with only a few pale stars showing through. So most people are forgetting what a starry sky looks like. Light pollution cuts us off from our view of the universe.

You *must* get away from lights as much as you can. Most of us cannot get right away from them, except when camping in the mountains or the desert. The farther you can get from cities (and highways and houses), the darker will be your sky, and the more stars you'll see.

A test of a good sky is whether you can see the Milky Way. In earlier times, people even in cities were used to the sight of it.

Trees, mountains, and clouds are not as bad as—   light pollution.

The naked eye

Your "naked eyes" are your eyes without aid, except for eyeglasses if you wear those.

Observing with naked eyes may be all you ever want to do. You can see much more this way than many people realize: the Moon, five planets, up to three thousand stars, the Milky Way, and another galaxy (Andromeda; see the November page) which is more than two million light-years away. You can learn the constellations, make scientific counts of meteors, and point to many things that look like stars but are clusters or nebulae. Telescopes were invented only in 1608. The science of astronomy had progressed a long way without them.

All astronomers need to start with a firm grasp of naked-eye astronomy. Some of the greatest astronomers regularly go back to gazing at the sky for pleasure and inspiration.

Binoculars

Get binoculars before you think of getting a telescope.

They cost much less. As well as using them on the night sky, you can enjoy them in the daytime, looking at landscapes, birds, or ships. They are small for carrying around. They are easy to use: you just line them up with where your eyes are looking (which is *not* all you need to do with a telescope). Things appear the same way around (whereas in many telescopes for astronomy they appear upside down). You use both eyes, which makes things seem more real. Binoculars are like powerful eyes: you look at the Pleiades, and see scores of stars instead of six. Binoculars have a much wider field of view than telescopes, so you do not find yourself lost in the spaces between stars. You can explore with them along the Milky Way and keep discovering beautiful sights. For hazy objects such as the Great Orion Nebula, binoculars are in a way *better* than telescopes, which spread out the misty light so much that it is hard to see.

People who go on to use telescopes keep and use binoculars too.

Even the cheapest binoculars will give you an amazingly good view. The trouble with cheap ones is that they may be spoiled the first time you drop them. The ordinary, all-purpose size of binoculars is called "7×35," which means they magnify 7 times and the lenses are 35 millimeters wide. Bigger ones show dimmer stars, but are hard to hold steady.

Telescopes

Going further into astronomy means using a telescope. You need it if you are to see (*really* see, not just in someone else's photos)
- Jupiter's bands and colors
- Saturn's separate rings
- satellites around the planets
- asteroids
- double stars
- the fine details of a comet's tail or the Orion Nebula
- distant galaxies . . .

A telescope gives you a magnified view of a tiny piece of the sky. You can easily point it at a few things you can see already, such as the Moon. After that, you are in trouble. There are myriads of other things to see, but they are lost in the dark spaces between naked-eye stars. To find them you have to use astronomical maps and "right ascension," "declination," "setting circles" or "go-to" software—things you haven't yet heard of.

I wouldn't want to discourage you from getting a telescope. You may have been given one for Christmas. Just realize that, to put it to use, you are going to have to learn some more from other books—or people.

Look at the articles and ads in magazines such as *Sky & Telescope* or *Astronomy*. Talk with a science teacher, or any other astro nut you happen to know. Best of all, find the nearest astronomy club, join it—and people will probably fall over each other offering you advice and letting you look through their scopes.

So that you can understand your astro friends' chatter

A telescope works by gathering light, with either a lens or a mirror. It gathers much more light than just your eye can, by being wider; that's how it lets us see much dimmer stars.

(So a word you'll hear is **aperture**, which means "opening." An ordinary amateur telescope may have a mirror 6 inches wide; the giant Keck telescope has an aperture of 10 meters—33 feet.)

Then the telescope brings this light to a **focus** by refracting the light through the lens, or reflecting it off the curved mirror. So the two main kinds of telescope are *refractors*, the earliest kind, and **reflectors**, which are more common now.

Usually the light has to go through a pathway of one or two other lenses or mirrors to get it conveniently to the **eyepiece**, a lens that finally focuses it in your eye.

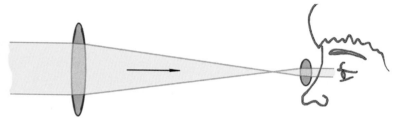

Light coming through the lens of a refracting telescope
(like the kind made by Galileo in 1609)

or bouncing off the main mirror,
in one kind of reflecting telescope
(the kind first made by Isaac Newton in 1668)

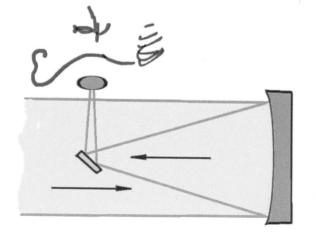

VARIOUS MATTERS

Astronomy

comes from the Greek words *aster*, "star," and *nomos*, "law." So it meant the study of how the stars are arranged. We now know that there are many other things out in space, so astronomy is the study of them all. It covers everything in the universe. Most other subjects (such as geography, botany, history) are concerned with things on our small planet, the Earth.

You can see only a small bit of this small planet at one time, because it is a solid ball and you live at a spot on its surface. But you can see half the universe in one glance, just by looking up at the night sky!

This makes astronomy easier than geography, in a way. You can only see other parts of the Earth by looking at pictures or maps. In astronomy besides using pictures and maps you can look straight out at the real thing.

—is NOT astrology

Set people right when they say (they will!) "Oh, you're interested in astrology." The two words have come to be applied to different things. Astronomy is a science that tries to find out real facts about the universe. Astrology is a set of ancient beliefs about how the positions of the Sun, Moon, and planets may affect people's characters and luck.

Names

Sometimes it may seem as if you start out wanting to learn about the stars, and find yourself having to learn languages instead! You could think of it as a nuisance, or you could think of it as an extra bit of interest that you get from astronomy.

Our constellation names are in **Latin**. (All the oldest ones came from **Greek**, but they are now written in a Latin way.)

Some of the stars' names are Greek and Latin too, such as *Sirius* and *Spica*. Many others are **Arabic**, or, at least, they are corruptions of Arabic words. This happened because in the Middle Ages the Arabs were writing many books about astronomy while there was not much of it going on in Europe.

Constellations

Stella is the Latin word for "star," and constellations are groups of stars. They are our way of finding places in the sky.

You could make groups out of the stars in different ways. The peoples of the world, such as the Chinese or the native tribes of America, had their own constellations. Some of those we now use probably started with the ancient Babylonians. The Greeks took them over and added to them, and a Greek astronomer called Ptolemy drew up a list of 48 constellations. These include most of the ones we have shown you in this book.

Around 1500 A.D. European explorers invented new constellations in the southern part of the sky which the Greeks had never seen. Also, European astronomers felt free to invent new constellations in the spaces between the old ones. Some of these invented constellations dropped out of use (such as Quadrans, which we mentioned because it gave its name to the Quadrantid meteor shower). In the end, 88 official constellations were agreed on.

Constellations started as just patterns made by a few brighter stars. For instance, one part of the sky has some stars that, if you imagine lines between them, remind you of a lion, so that's the constellation Leo. This is just the way it looks from Earth; the stars aren't really close to each other in space, some being much farther away than others.

But what about all the fainter stars and other details? To refer to them, they had to be "in" constellations. So in 1930 official boundaries were drawn, and every part of the sky is in one of the 88 constellations. Constellations started as dot-pictures made with a few stars, but they have become areas of the sky, like countries.

Greek letters

It's nice to use names for the stars, like "Capella" and "Altair," but it's not enough. Only a few bright stars have names, but many faint stars turn out to be interesting, and there has to be a way of referring to them.

In 1603 Johann Bayer started using Greek letters. For instance Regulus, being the brightest star in Leo, is called **α** of that constellation; Denebola, the second brightest, is **β**; and some others get **γ**, **δ**, and so on.

The proper way is to say for instance "α Leonis" (or "Alpha Leonis"). **Leo** is Latin for "lion"; **Leonis** is the possessive form of it, so that α **Leonis** means "α of the Lion." Back then, there was no difficulty about this: all educated people knew Greek and Latin! Now you can either learn a little Latin, or take the easy way and say "Alpha of Leo."

Here is a table of the Greek letters and their names:

α alpha	ι iota	ρ rho
β beta	κ kappa	σ sigma
γ gamma	λ lambda	τ tau
δ delta	μ mu	υ upsilon
ε epsilon	ν nu	φ phi
ζ zeta	ξ xi	χ chi
η eta	ο omicron	ψ psi
θ theta	π pi	ω omega

A constellation (guess which!), showing the imaginary picture its bright stars make, and its official boundary.

The astronomers who drew up these lines tried to make sure that each star was in the constellation it was traditionally supposed to be in.

Distances

Knowing how far away things are in space is very interesting and important. The trouble is, the distances are so enormous. And there are so many of them that get mentioned.

I suggest you fix in your mind just three basic, rough distances, in miles:

width of the Earth	**8,000**
Earth to Sun	**93,000,000**
light-year	**6,000,000,000,000**

Say them as "eight thousand miles," "ninety-three million miles," and "six million million miles."

Hang onto these, and think of other distances in terms of them. You needn't try to remember the other distances; just picture to yourself roughly how large they are.

(1) **The width of the Earth**, or

Earth-width for short. The Moon is about 30 Earth-widths away. And the Moon is a bit more than ¼ of an Earth-width wide. The largest planet, Jupiter, is about 11 Earth-widths wide. The Sun is 109 Earth-widths wide.

(2) **The Earth-to-Sun distance.** This is useful for measuring distances between things in the solar system—from Earth to another planet, from the Sun to a comet, and so on. It is the unit that astronomers regularly use for all this, so they have a name for it: the "**astronomical unit**." Here are the distances of

Mercury	0.4	Jupiter	5.2
Venus	0.7	Saturn	9.5
Earth	1	Uranus	19
Mars	1.5	Neptune	30

the planets outward from the Sun, in astronomical units: This makes it easy to see that Mercury is less than half our dis-

tance from the Sun and Jupiter is about 5 times farther out than us.

Here's a question with a surprising answer: which planet is nearest to *half* way out to Neptune? (Answer: Uranus.)

(3) **The light-year.** Always remember that this is a distance, not a time! It is the distance that light travels in one year. Light is the fastest thing there is. It travels at an incredible speed: 186,000 miles per second! This means that the light-year, the distance light travels in a whole year, is a fantastically large distance.

The light-year is used for distances between stars and galaxies. We've mentioned the distances of some things as we talked about them: the nearest star, a bit more than 4 light-years, for example; Sirius, about 9; Deneb, perhaps 3,000. The Andromeda Galaxy, 2,500,000.

Picturing distances

Even the width of the Earth is far too large for us really to imagine. Yet the Earth-Sun distance is nearly 12,000 times larger than that! And the light-year is 64,000 times larger than the Earth-Sun distance.

It helps to think about a model or picture of these things. Remember that in the picture at the beginning of our "More Explanations" we drew the Earth 8/100 of an inch wide. This was about the smallest we could draw it. Now, suppose you want to draw this picture so as to include other things on the proper scale. What is that scale? It is 8/100 inch to 8,000 miles: 1/100 inch represents 1,000 miles. So:

—The Sun should be 26 yards away! (You already need a ridiculously long piece of paper.)

—To show a light-year you will have to draw a line 950 miles long!

—The nearest star should be more than 4 of these light-years away. So, if you live in the middle of the U.S., you will have to draw the nearest star in Iceland, or Bolivia, or Hawaii!

Here's the only way we can draw part of this picture on a page of the book:

Sun   *center of the Sun*

Earth   *Moon*

A picture of the distance from the Earth to the Sun. Straightened, the line would be 26 yards long.

Angles

You say to a friend: "Look at that star. It's the Double-Double star in Lyra." "I can't see where you're pointing. Which star?" "The one that's not far left of Vega." "*How* far left of Vega?" "Oh, about two inches." Finally your friend understands which star you mean, but says: "I think it must be at least *twenty light-years* left of Vega." Which of you is right?

Neither. You can't possibly know how far one star is from the other in **linear measure** (inches, miles, light-years) unless you know how far away they both are. The distance you are really talking about is in **angular measure**, and it is measured in degrees.

For instance, look at something straight in front of you. Now turn your head to look at something straight to the left of you. You have turned your head through 90 degrees.

You should have said, perhaps, "The star about two degrees left of Vega." But how do you measure these angles in the sky? Since they aren't in inches or centimeters, you can't hold up a ruler to them. Here is a useful rough way of doing it:

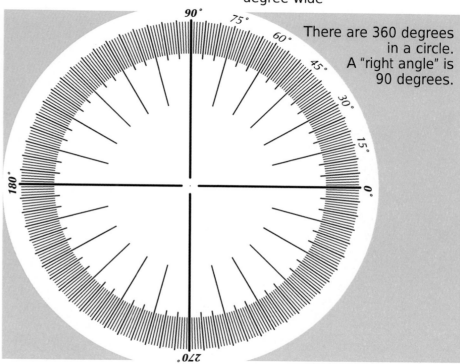

A (thumbless) handspan

Hold your arm out straight, stretching it to get your hand *as far away from your eye as possible*. Now (keeping your thumb tucked in) stretch your little finger and your index finger as far apart as possible. The angle you see, from the tip of your little finger to the tip of your index finger, is about 15 degrees.

From this you can also estimate 30 degrees (two of these handspans) or 5 degrees (a third of a handspan).

(A full handspan from thumb to little finger is about 20 degrees.)

A useful thing about the thumbless handspan is that 15 degrees is the distance the Sun moves to the right in one hour. So, if somebody says "I wonder how long we've got till sunset," you can stretch out your arm, measure how many thumbless handspans it is from the Sun to the place where it will set, and announce "Two and a half hours!" (You'll be able to do this *if* you know roughly where the Sun is going to set, from having watched it before.)

Look at Orion (as in the January pages). His two shoulder stars are about 7.5 degrees apart—*half* of a thumbless handspan. One hour later, the stars will have moved 15 degrees in the direction of the arrow (that is, westward).

Pinkie-thickness

Here is an even easier method, though it is only for smaller angles. Hold up just your little finger, as far as you can get it from your eye. It appears *one* degree wide.

How wide do you think the Moon looks? Make a guess. Five degrees? Test your guess when you can actually see the Moon: hold your outstretched little finger up in front of it. You will find that the Moon is only half as wide as your little finger; it's only half a degree wide! This is surprising. The Moon looks bright and important up there, and in paintings it's usually shown much wider than it really is.

If you make the same test on the Sun, you'll have to do it *very* quickly—**never look at the Sun for more than a split second (it's better not to look directly at it at all)**. The Sun looks almost exactly the same width as the Moon, half a degree.

This shows you the difference between angular and linear size. The Moon and Sun "look" the same size, but they "are really" very different. The Sun is really 400 times wider than the Moon; but it is also 400 times farther away, so they both appear half a degree wide

There are 360 degrees in a circle. A "right angle" is 90 degrees.

GLOSSARY

Here are most but not all of the names and special words we have mentioned. Their pronunciations are shown in brackets [ ]. Many of the names can be pronounced differently; for instance, American and British people have different pronunciations. It doesn't really matter!

Achernar [*AK-er-nar*]: a bright star.
Aldebaran [*al-DEB-a-ran*]: a bright reddish star.
Alcyone [*al-SY-o-nee*]: a star, one of the Pleiades.
Algol [*AL-gol*]: a variable star.
Altair [*al-TAIR*]: a bright star.
Andromeda [*an-DROM-e-da*]: a constellation (name of a princess).
Antares [*an-TAIR-eez*]: a bright reddish star.
Aquarius [*a-KWAIR-i-us*]: "water-carrier," a constellation.
Aquila [*AK-wi-la*]: "eagle," a constellation.
Arcturus [*ark-TUE-rus*]: a bright star.
Aries [*AIR-i-eez*]: "ram," a constellation.
asteroid: one of the thousands of "small planets" that go around the Sun, besides the eight major planets.
Auriga [*OR-i-ga*]: "charioteer," a constellation.
Berenice [*be-re-NY-see*]: a queen. See Coma Berenices.
Betelgeuse [*BET-el-jooz*]: a bright reddish star.
Boötes [*bo-O-teez*]: "herdsman," a constellation.
Cancer [*KAN-ser*]: "crab," a constellation.
Canis Major [*KAY-nis MAY-jor*]: "greater dog," a constellation.
Canopus [*ka-NO-pus*]: a bright star.
Capella [*ka-PELL-a*]: a bright star.
Capricornus [*kap-ri-KORN-us*]: "goat," a constellation.
Cassiopeia [*kass-i-o-PEE-a*]: a constellation (name of a queen).
Castor [*KASS-tor*]: a bright star.
Centaurus [*sen-TOR-us*]: a constellation.
Cepheus [*SEE-fewce*]: a constellation (name of a king).

Cetus [*SEE-tus*]: "whale," a constellation.
Coma Berenices [*KOE-ma be-re-NY-seez*]: "hair of Berenice," a constellation.
constellation: a group of stars that form a picture, and mark an area of the sky.
Corona Borealis [*ko-ROE-na bor-ee-AY-lis*]: "northern crown," a constellation.
Cygnus [*SIG-nus*]: "swan," a constellation.
Delphinus [*del-FY-nus*]: "dolphin," a constellation.
Deneb [*DEN-eb*]: a bright star.
Draco [*DRAY-koe*]: "dragon," a constellation.
ecliptic [*e-KLIP-tik*]: imaginary line in the sky along which the Sun moves. It is really the plane in which the Earth revolves around the Sun.
equator [*e-KWAY-tor*]: imaginary line around the middle of the Earth, dividing it into northern and southern hemispheres. Above it is the **celestial equator** ("sky equator"), which we often call just "equator" too, dividing the northern and southern halves of the sky.
equinoxes [*EEK-wi-nok-siz*]: the two times (in March and September) when the Sun crosses the equator.
Eridanus [*e-ri-DAY-nus*]: a constellation (name of a river).
Fomalhaut [*FOM-al-hawt* or *FO-ma-lo*]: a bright star.
galaxy: a huge collection of stars (and other objects such as nebulae). The Sun is one of the stars in the Milky Way galaxy.
Gemini [*JEM-i-nye*]: "twins," a constellation.
Hercules [*HUR-cue-leez*]: a constellation (name of a hero).
Hyades [*HY-a-deez*]: a cluster of stars.
Hydra [*HY-dra*]: "water-serpent," a constellation.
Kokab [*KOE-kab*]: a star near the Pole Star.
Leo [*LEE-oh*]: "lion," a constellation.
Libra [*LY-bra*]: "scales" (for weighing), a constellation.
Lyra [*LY-ra*]: "lyre," a constellation.
Medusa [*med-YOU-za*]: a mythical woman in the story of Perseus.

meteor [*MEE-tee-or*]: a flash of light in the sky, caused by a bit of dust, sand or rock striking the Earth's atmosphere.

meteorite [*MEE-tee-or-ite*]: a piece of rock that is found on Earth, having fallen from space.

Milky Way: the galaxy we live in; our Sun is one of the billions of stars in it. It looks to us like a band of soft light stretching all around the sky.

Mira [*MY-ra*]: a variable star.

nebula [*NEB-you-la*]: a misty patch of light. Some nebulas (or nebulae) are huge clouds of gas or dust in space, much larger than stars. Others that used to be called nebulae are now known to be really **galaxies**.

Ophiuchus [*o-fi-OO-kus*]: "snake-holder," a constellation.

orbit: the path that a body, such as a planet, travels around another body, such as the Sun. Usually it has the shape of an ellipse.

Orion [*o-RY-an*]: a constellation (name of a hunter).

Pegasus [*PEG-a-sus*]: a constellation (name of a flying horse).

Perseids [*PER-see-idz*]: a shower of meteors in August.

Perseus [*PER-sewce*]: a constellation (name of a hero).

Pisces [*PY-seez*]: "fishes," a constellation.

Piscis Austrinus [*PY-siss aw-STRY-nus*]: "southern fish," a constellation.

Pleiades [*PLY-a-deez* or *PLEE-a-deez*]: a cluster of stars.

Pollux [*POLL-ux*]: a bright star.

Praesepe [*pree-SEE-pee*]: "manger," a cluster of stars, also called the Beehive.

Procyon [*pro-SY-on*]: a star.

Proserpina [*pro-SUR-pin-a*], also called **Persephone** [*pur-SEFF-o-nee*]: the girl in the story told about the constellation Virgo (June).

Proxima Centauri: the nearest star, a small companion to Alpha Centauri. *Proxima* means "nearest" in Latin.

Regulus [*REG-you-lus*]: a bright star.

Rigel [*RY-jel*]: a bright star.

Sagittarius [*saj-i-TAIR-i-us*]: "archer," a constellation.

Scorpius [*SKOR-pi-us*] or **Scorpio**: "scorpion," a constellation.

Serpens [*SER-penz*]: "snake," a constellation. It is in two separated parts, Serpens Cauda and Serpens Caput, meaning "snake tail" and "snake head."

Sirius [*SIRR-i-us*]: the brightest star.

solstices [*SOL-stiss-iz*]: the time in June when the Sun is farthest north in the sky, and the time in December when it is farthest south.

Spica [*SPY-ka*]: a bright star.

Taurus [*TOR-us*]: "bull," a constellation.

Triangulum [*try-ANG-you-lum*]: "triangle," a constellation.

Uranus [*you-RAIN-us* or *YOU-run-us*]: the 7th planet.

Ursa Major [*UR-sa MAY-jor*]: "greater bear," a constellation.

Vega [*VEE-ga*]: a bright star.

Virgo [*VUR-go*]: "virgin," a constellation.

Vulpecula [*vul-PECK-you-la*]: "fox," a constellation.

zenith [*ZEN-ith* or *ZEEN-ith*]: the direction straight above your head.

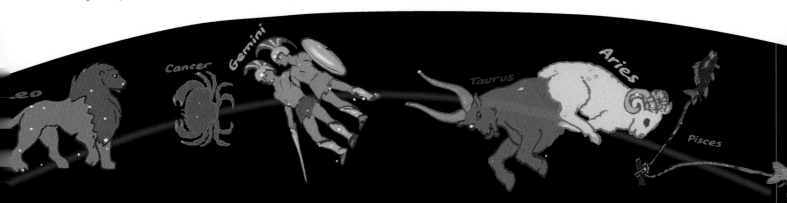

zodiac [*ZO-dee-ak*]: the twelve constellations through which the ecliptic runs.

Made in the USA
San Bernardino, CA
12 December 2014